stepping off the beaten path

IN PURSUIT OF JESUS

RICK AND BEV LAWRENCE

Group

LOVELAND, COLORADO
www.group.com

In Pursuit of Jesus
Copyright © 2008 Rick and Bev Lawrence

Visit our Web site: **www.group.com**

Credits
Editor: Brad Lewis
Developer: Roxanne Wieman
Project Manager: Scott M. Kinner
Chief Creative Officer: Joani Schultz
Copy Editor: Dena Twinem
Art Director: Jeff Storm
Print Production Artist: The DesignWorks Group, Inc.
Cover Art Director/Designer: Jeff Storm
Production Manager: DeAnne Lear

ISBN: 978-0-7644-3677-2

10 9 8 7 6 5 4 3 2 1   17 16 15 14 13 12 11 10 09 08

ACKNOWLEDGMENTS

First, we'd like to thank Jesus, who romanced us into pursuing him in the first place—we (only) love because he loved us first.

Second, we'd like to thank all the people who took a chance and gave in to their curiosity and thirst to show up to a study that was way out of the box for many. We treasure your tears, your laughter, your life-changing insights, and the sense of "family" you brought to this pursuit.

Third, we'd like to thank our daughters, Lucy and Emma, who got up early on Sunday, for so many Sundays, so we could teach this study. For Lucy, who ended up actually participating in the class and adding profound insights—we loved your presence with us. For Emma, who had to hear Dad say, "Not right now, honey" about a thousand times while I finished preparing this study for publication—we appreciate your patience with us.

Fourth, we'd like to thank the leaders in our church—particularly Bob Krulish, Anthony Vartuli, and Tom Melton—who believe in Jesus, us, and this study.

IN PURSUIT OF JESUS

DEDICATION

To our dear daughters, Lucy and Emma.
Our prayers over you have always been that you would have
hearts that burn for Jesus. As you grow,
we hope he's more and more your consuming passion.
We love you, dears.

IN PURSUIT OF JESUS

CONTENTS

IN PURSUIT OF JESUS

INTRODUCTION

We birthed this 10-week adventure into the heart of Jesus out of passion and desperation. At the time, we had no thoughts of anyone other than us leading people on this pursuit. After years of going to church classes and small groups that tried to focus on Jesus and the great truths of Scripture, we felt unsatisfied with our experiences. In those learning environments, we often felt like we'd been invited to a feast at a friend's house, but when we showed up, we found crackers and cheese as the main course. Sure, we ate something, but it was no feast.

We were hungry for more. More of Jesus.

In fact, we *had to* have more of Jesus. We needed him like two thirsty survivors crawling toward a well in the desert. So we decided to create the kind of study we wished we could go to. We came up with 10 "snapshots" of Jesus that seemed worth pursuing. Then we plunged ourselves into each one with a determination not just to get at the truth of Jesus, but to do so in an engaging, experiential, and interactive way that also honored what participants in the class would bring to the table.

We set before ourselves and the "family" that ended up attending this class the overarching question that Jesus asked his disciples after the feeding of the 5,000 (Luke 9:12-20): "Who do you say I am?" Our simple mission: Spend 10 weeks exploring our answer to that question. Further, we wanted to go beyond answering that question only with our heads; we very much wanted to respond to the question with our hearts.

You can understand the truth about Jesus in a lot of different ways—just as you can understand the truth about your spouse or best friend in different ways. Not all of these ways have to do with hard facts; many have to do more with your "heart knowledge" of the person. The reason you marry someone or hang out with someone has as much to do with your emotional experience (your heart knowledge) as your "factual" assessment of who someone is.

So we decided not to "market" the class to our church in the typical way, with announcements from the pulpit and a pleading sales pitch in the bulletin. Instead, we placed the following notice in the bulletin—the only place we publicized the class:

IN PURSUIT OF JESUS

A new class just for the summer. No tips and techniques. No life application. No homework. No acronyms. Just Jesus. All ages welcome! Taught by Rick and Bev Lawrence.

When only five people showed up for our first class, Bev was sure I'd made an arrogant, boneheaded mistake (by the way, whenever you read "I" in these introductory pages, it's Rick talking unless we tell you otherwise). Still, something within me simply wanted to cast a net for people who were desperate enough for Jesus to be intrigued by our terse bulletin announcement.

Somewhere along the way, we collected about 30 regulars who journeyed with us through the class. At the end of our time together, we asked people to write about how the experience affected them. The depth and breadth of the transformation they reported astonished us. Here are a few samples:

- ▶ "The teaching was both profound and easy to understand. I have a better, deeper love for Jesus because of better knowledge and understanding of him."
- ▶ "I loved digging deeper and thinking. I was welcomed. I had a voice. Thank you."
- ▶ "The class really helped me get to know Jesus and helped me to be a follower of Jesus…You don't have any idea how much this class has done for me. Thank you so much!"
- ▶ "I now feel more intimate in my relationship with Jesus. I liked the deep exploration in the class. It left me wanting more of the class—and him!"
- ▶ "No acronyms, no applications, no techniques! I loved the way you used music, film, discussion—all different aspects."
- ▶ "Excellent subjects, teaching, and facilitating! Also loved the fellowships and varied activities. The preparation, teaching, subjects, discussion, activities, fellowship, and new friends all made a big impact on my life."

▶ "I can grow when the ground is plowed deeper. I liked the questions that made me look at truths in a new light."

▶ "I felt as though I was on holy ground. I felt challenged and encouraged."

CLASS OR SMALL GROUP?

▶ While we've taught this material as a Sunday school class, it works equally well as a study in a small-group setting.

After the pursuit was over and we had a chance to catch our breath, we realized we'd been a part of something powerful. When we saw people who'd attended the class in the hallways at church—a wide spectrum of participants from teenagers to senior adults—they stopped us with a kind of a hunger in their eyes to ask when we planned to offer the class again. Many expressed that for the first time, their insights and input were passionately valued in the study. We not only gave participants the opportunity to think more critically and make their own discoveries about Jesus, we kind of forced them to do it. And they loved it because they "owned" it! They loved the atmosphere of participation, dignity, and respect that grew up around our joint pursuit.

WHY THIS CLASS WORKS

I think the best metaphor for a typical class or small-group study is a jet—one pilot controls pretty much everything about the craft's navigation, and a lot of passengers just go along for the ride.

The metaphor that best describes this series is a viking ship—the ship has a captain (you, the leader), but *everyone* rows. Each individual helps determine how far, how fast, and what direction the ship heads. The captain provides strong leadership, overarching direction, expert navigational insight, and prods the rowers to row. And when you get to your destination in a viking ship, everyone feels the satisfaction of playing a key role in the journey. Of course, that's not the case with passengers on a jet.

We first led this class in the summer of 2006. That fall, Joani Schultz (the Chief Creative Officer at Group Publishing, where I've worked for 20 years), asked about the best part of my summer. I could barely wait to answer, and blurted out, "The 'In Pursuit of Jesus' class Bev and I taught!" Joani listened to me excitedly describe the impact of the class, then—with her characteristic enthusiasm—said, "We've got to get this published so others can do it!"

You now hold the result of that conversation in your hands.

Bev and I believe that true transformation comes when you get closer to Jesus. We feel so strongly about this, I'm tempted to just write that sentence again:

We believe that true transformation comes when you get closer to Jesus.

The aim of this pursuit isn't just to get closer to Jesus, but to get infected by him. To move him from the fringes of everyday life to the bull's-eye of everyday life.

As you prepare to launch into this adventure, know that we're with you. We couldn't be more excited about the journey you're about to take!

—RICK AND BEV LAWRENCE

IN PURSUIT OF JESUS

BOOT CAMP FOR LEADING THIS PURSUIT

This 10-week pursuit probably differs from most studies you've led. Even if that's not the case, we've learned some vital insights over the years for leading study times that involve a lot of interactions, debriefing, and feedback. Instead of a lecture or fill-in-the-blank style—strategies that have questionable long-term impact on participants—we use music, film, high-octane discussions, and experiences to get at the core truths about Jesus. This is a really fun, amazing way to lead people into deeper learning. Once you've led this way, you'll never go back to the one-way communication methods most of us have tried.

Let's explore what makes this series different, and what you can expect as the leader.

LEADING AS A TEAM

We've always team-taught this study with Rick taking the lead role and Bev jumping in with responses or taking portions she feels compelled to lead. However, we've designed this leaders guide for an individual to lead participants through the studies.

THE LEADER'S ROLE

In a typical small-group or Sunday school study, a leader talks almost all the time. Sometimes, a couple of discussion questions get tossed out, but they're often a sidelight to the real meat of the study.

In this series, the leader talks, but the participants talk, too. A lot. If you're leading this series, you'll feel more like a ringmaster than a lecturer. You'll offer strong leadership in a context where many people participate and add to the content of the study.

Allow us to explain why that's such a great thing.

First, research shows that people learn best by *doing*. In fact, the people who learn the most in classrooms are the teachers—because they first need to ingest what they're teaching before they teach it. So what happens when people get immersed in experiences and talk to each other (and you) about what they're learning while they're learning it? Well, real learning takes place.

If you're a curious person who likes good conversation and who knows how to ask follow-up questions, you'll thrive in this learning environment. If you don't think you have any of these qualities, don't worry. We've tried to craft instructions for these sessions in a way that allows anyone to lead them. You simply need to see your role as a strong leader who has opinions but who wants to hear the experiences and opinions of others as well.

Of course, the most important aspect of leading this study is to let it transform you *first*. As you prepare to lead, you need to pursue the questions and insights first. In essence, that's what being a leader means…going first. In this study, the leader provides important insights. Right now, these insights are all in our voice. You could say them just as we've written them for you. But of course, you don't want to mimic our voice when you lead this series—everything must filter through who you are. But you *do* want to make sure to understand and own these insights—by the time you lead each study, you'll have explored it for yourself first and let it impact you.

"SAY SOMETHING LIKE:"

Throughout this study, we've placed the words you need to say in bold. This allows them to stand out, and you can easily scan for what you need to say.

USING THE PURSUIT OF JESUS WEB SITE

We've set up a special Web site just for leaders of this study series—it's www.pursuitof jesus.com. Go there and you'll find links to Web resources you'll need, including videos, songs, and lyrics. And to help you capture the spirit and dynamics of leading this study, we videotaped a session and put it on the site—just click and watch. You can also toss us your questions and ask for advice or even give feedback.

THE PERSONAL JOURNEY GUIDE

Each student in your class will need an *In Pursuit of Jesus Personal Journey Guide* (available from Group Publishing at www.group.com and at your local Christian retailer). These *Personal Journey Guides* are an integral part of your time together. The guides lead small groups through discussion, ask compelling questions, and provide people with the resources they need to explore each weekly topic. The guides also serve as a journal for each participant; there's lots of room for taking notes, writing personal insights, and answering questions. Encourage participants to use the guides regularly during your times together.

WELCOME

In each study, we simply urge you to welcome everyone at the start. When we lead the study, we usually make this short: "Welcome to the study, we're glad you're here. Today we'll be focusing on..." You don't need to do much more than that to make people feel welcome because the whole study involves a lot of relational activity and story-sharing. People will get to know each other well as they interact with one another. If you like, you can also briefly mention the overarching question you'll be pursuing: Jesus asked, "Who do you say I am?" And you can mention the main theme of the previous study, along with a very brief overview for those who might have missed it.

MUSIC

You'll use music quite a bit in this series of studies. Each music suggestion has a specific purpose. That doesn't mean you can't substitute other music in place of what we suggest—or even do away with the music completely (although we don't recommend that). The music makes the experience richer. If you're computer-literate, you can easily find the suggested music online and pay to download them (from iTunes, for example; you can burn songs to a CD if you have that capability). Or simply play the songs off your computer (go to a site such as www.rhapsody.com and search for the suggested songs). A third option is buying the CDs (look for cheap used versions on Amazon.com) so you can enjoy some of the greatest music ever made.

If you take this route, you'll need to buy or borrow these albums:

- ▶ *Love and Thunder* by Andrew Peterson (Essential, 2003)
- ▶ *Behold the Lamb of God* by Andrew Peterson (Fervent Records, 2004)
- ▶ *The Life,* Disc 1 and Disc 2 by Michael Card (Sparrow, 1988)
- ▶ *Add to the Beauty* by Sara Groves (Ino, 2005)
- ▶ *All That You Can't Leave Behind* by U2 (Interscope, 2000)
- ▶ *The Ministry Years 1980-1982* by Keith Green (Sparrow, 1988)
- ▶ *Arriving* by Chris Tomlin (Sparrow, 2004)
- ▶ *The World as Best as I Remember It Vol. 1* by Rich Mullins (Reunion, 1991)

We've made it easy for you by linking to the songs you'll need on our Web site—www.pursuitofjesus.com.

Also, we've created a summary for each song we use in the study. It's difficult to get permission to put the actual lyrics in the Leaders Guide and Personal Journey Guide—so we simply summarized the songs so you and your group members can get an overview of the lyrics as you listen to or debrief the songs. If you'd like to print out the actual lyrics, we've put links to each song's lyrics on our Web site—www.pursuitofjesus.com.

One other note about music: We suggest playing soft and unobtrusive instrumental music (most often jazz) as a background during discussion times. It creates a kind of colorful backdrop and juxtaposition to the sometimes intense discussions. Just keep an instrumental CD in the boombox, and push play or pause at the beginning and end of each discussion. Music helps set the mood and provides a powerful entry point into people's hearts. Because this study engages both the head and the heart, music plays a crucial role in helping people open their hearts to Jesus.

FILM

You'll also use film clips quite a bit throughout the series. Film functions as a "third person in the room." In other words, people often find it easier to respond to a scene from a film than to a statement you make. Responding to a film clip offers a safe way for people to express their opinions. In addition, film serves as a powerful storytelling medium—nearly everyone will engage with a film clip. This means the clips you show function just like the parables Jesus told. You'll use film clips to set up topics, as parables that connect to some aspect of Jesus, and as allegories that flesh out biblical truths.

Be sure to cue up the clips, set the volume, and test your electronics before people arrive for the session. If you're fiddling with equipment while people arrive, you basically greet them with your backside. At best, this means you're distracted as you talk with them.

Don't assume that everyone in the room has seen the film you're using. When you get to the point in a study when you show a clip, briefly set up the scene participants will watch. We provide the setup when you need it. On rare occasions that we don't provide the setup, just play the scene without explanation. Of course, you still should watch the scene first and make sure you understand the beginning and ending cues. Last, if your DVD player has a subtitle function that you can turn on and off, turn it on for your clips, just to help people catch any dialogue they might miss otherwise.

THUMBS UP

If you haven't seen the movies we've chosen clips from, we encourage you to watch the whole film in advance of that week's session. What a great excuse to watch some amazing films!

EXPERIENCES

Many of the sessions in this series include experiences that participants will do and you'll then "debrief." By "experiences," we mean activities that require everyone to participate, not just sit back and listen. These might be fun, meditative, or mildly uncomfortable. But the goal is to lead people into activities where they feel fully engaged.

Debriefing is just another way of saying that you will artfully engage participants with good initial questions about the experience, followed by good follow-up questions. You help the people in your group build bridges from unforgettable experiences to unforgettable truths. When you succeed, you can truly say two things: you've "taught," and the participants have "learned."

These experiences aren't just fringe illustrations or funky gimmicks. Research shows that people learn more deeply through direct experiences than any other teaching approach. You might be tempted to think lightly of these experiences, or diminish them, or cut them out if you're pressed for time. But don't give in to temptation! We know not just from research but from decades of personal experience in teaching this way, that good experiences—debriefed well by a leader—hold unmatched power to capture and change people.

We urge you to pay close attention to the details of these experiences so you can easily give instructions to participants. We provide clear and specific direction on how to set up, lead, and debrief these experiences. A leader can ruin a great experience by leaving out a crucial step, giving fuzzy directions, or not grasping the makeup of the experience itself. Even more, you'll torpedo a powerful experience if you "hedge your bets" by apologizing for or diminishing an experience in your setup for it. If you doubt that people will get much out of the experience, suspend your disbelief and just decide to believe people will do what you ask them to do. We can tell you, they will. And they'll remember the experiences years from now.

We'll talk a little more about what to cut and not cut from each session if, for some reason, time is tight. But our general rule of thumb is never cut an experience. Instead, cut down on what you say. As much as we want to just tell people what we think they should know, a good experience will teach people a lesson they'll never forget. Keep in mind that the experiences in this pursuit aren't just "illustrations" or "object lessons"; they're the very meat of the study. So, more than any other aspect of this series, make sure you understand and are ready to lead the experiences.

PLAY WITH US!

We often lead people into experiences by asking them to just "play with us." I often catch myself saying something like: "There's nothing on the line here. We're just going to experiment with something, and I'd love for you to put in the clutch on your skepticism and just go with it. I'm really just telling you to do what I say…with a smile on my face. Play, because God loves it when we do."

This gives people permission to be uncomfortable, but clearly communicates that you won't give them an "out." When you tell them to play instead of "work," you also lessen the intensity and allow them to really experience the experience.

DISCUSSIONS

At the heart of this series, you'll need to make a commitment to spark great discussions. As with any great discussion, you won't always be sure which way a conversation will go. You might be tempted to impose your will or your agenda on every discussion, but (for the most part) it's good to resist that temptation. Your goal should be to get every person contributing to the life and content of the sessions.

Sometimes people want to follow rabbit trails—directions that stray from your plan and threaten to hijack the carefully crafted teaching thread. Often, you'll want to follow rabbit trails—as long as the trail leads toward the overarching goal of answering Jesus' question: "Who do you say I am?" Occasionally, a participant might take over and force the study in a different, and ultimately unimportant, direction. When you sense you're getting bogged down in an interesting but unhelpful rabbit trail, stop walking down it and return to the main path.

HIJACKED!

If you aren't sure whether a discussion is a helpful rabbit trail or a blatant hijacking, ask yourself: "Is this leading us toward the overall goal of answering Jesus' question, 'Who do you say I am?' " If the answer is "no," you've been hijacked, and you need to gently but firmly and quickly guide the discussion back to focusing only on answering that main question.

We give you helpful guidance throughout the study sessions in the form of "Rules of Engagement" reminders. You can quickly scan these reminders about how to start, fuel, and end vibrant conversations.

You'll also see tips on:

- ▶ how to follow up answers.
- ▶ how to choose the answers to follow up and the ones to leave alone.
- ▶ how to attach participants' answers back to your main point in each session.

The best tool you can bring to this study is your own passionate, persistent, and creative curiosity. If you hear someone use a word that's a "given," ask yourself if you really understand what the person meant. For example, when we were teaching a session in this series this last Sunday, one person in the class said, "God is a profound lover." Most of us would just leave that comment as it stood, but we asked: "What do you mean by the word 'profound'?" The person had to stop and consider what she really meant; this led to a deeper understanding of God's love for all of us. Asking this kind of observant follow-up question provides the lifeblood of this study series.

To lead this study series, you'll need a white board or big pad of paper to write a condensed version of what *every person* answers—this isn't a fringe aspect of the series, it's crucial. You'll see what we mean when you dive into the studies. The idea is to publicly record—in shortened form—what everyone says. This supercharges the learning climate in your group, because participants quickly realize that what they have to say is important enough to write down. Also, as you write down what everyone says, the rest of the group gets a chance to think critically about others' answers, to loop back to something said earlier, and to make connections between two or more disconnected answers. This is absolutely crucial to the tone and content of these studies.

Sometimes a participant will give an answer that is…well…just wrong. Or at the very least, a confusing or irrelevant answer. You'll want to try hard not to place value judgments on how people answer. So when someone offers an answer that's blatantly wrong, unclear, or confusing, try one of these approaches:

1. *Ask for clarification on the answer.* For example, you might simply say, "Could you tell me that another way? I didn't get what you were saying." As you ask for clarification, you help people rethink their answers, or force them to expose the underlying problem with their answer on their own.

2. *If clarification doesn't change the nature of the problem, restate the answer to either high-light the problem or, instead, make a connection to a truth.* This sounds a little weird, but your discussion will go much smoother if you understand this crucial skill. I typically do this by saying, "Let me just translate what you're saying through my own filters. I hear you saying _____."

   This example might help. In week 2, in the study titled "Jesus Defines 'Good,' " participants make a list of things they define as "good," and then come up with their own definition or criteria for "good." One guy in a class we recently led said his criteria for "good" is anything he feels passionately drawn to. I said something like: "So, to use an extreme example, if Hitler followed your definition he could redefine the slaughter of millions of Jews as good because he was passionately drawn to it." The guy stopped to chew on that, but then I said: "If I translate what you're saying through my own filters, I hear you saying that something deep within us is drawn to real goodness. Is that right?" He nodded his head vigorously. I call this "push-back." You don't take anything as self-evident—not because you like to start fights, but because lazy thinking keeps us from growing.

3. *If clarification and restating don't work, or aren't appropriate, gently challenge the an-swer.* Not long ago, while teaching week 4, "Jesus and the Desperate People," I asked why the disciples so quickly dropped their nets to follow Jesus when he asked them to. One woman quickly answered that Jesus is the Messiah, and the disciples were just being obedient. I gently said, "But these men had just met Jesus shortly before he called them. While they might have heard he was a teacher or even a prophet, they certainly hadn't embraced him as the Mes-siah at this point. So they must have had other reasons to be willing to drop

everything and follow him." She saw my point, and that fueled more curiosity and creative thinking in the group.

4. *If a wrong or confusing answer isn't worth the time or effort to engage, just write it on your white board or pad and move on.* The first three suggestions apply to answers that have some application to the study, even though there's something a little off about them. This tip applies to answers that are so off-center that they're not worth clarifying. You might say something like: "Hmmm…thanks for that." Then simply move on to the next answer.

When people give a really insightful or powerful answer, try following up those answers by:

▶ asking the person to "say more" about what he or she means.

▶ adding something about how the comment or answer is impacting you personally in the moment. For example, make a statement that starts with "That makes me think of…." or "That underlines an important truth…"

▶ inviting additional discussion by saying something like, "Who has something to add to what _____ is saying?" This keeps the discussion going and prevents you from lecturing or one participant from dominating the discussion.

The goal behind all this strategy is to make your group or class a safe and inviting place for people to add their voice to the conversation. Most people won't be used to this kind of freedom, so the way you respond to their answers will encourage them to either "put something on the table" or "keep safely locked up" what they have to give.

Throughout this series, you'll switch between many kinds of interactions: partners, trios, and whole-group discussions. These self-directed discussion groups will pursue specific questions from the participant guides. During these discussion times, you can participate in one of the groups (if your class is small) or monitor the discussions to keep them within the suggested time limits.

By the way, if your class includes spouses, separate them for these discussion times. Spouses often think they know one another's story so well that they don't listen as well as they might with someone they don't know well. In discussions, you want people to pursue Jesus together with curiosity, and sometimes that gets muted when spouses are together.

ENDING DISCUSSION TIMES

Two other quick pieces of advice:

1. When people discuss something in pairs or trios, give a warning before you end the discussion. Simply call out, in a loud enough voice to gain attention: "You have one minute left…one minute left!"
2. When you end a discussion and need people to focus on you again, just say something like: "Can I have your attention again, please?" Repeat it until you get it.

Remember, you serve as the chief purveyor of curiosity and follow-up questions. You wield tremendous influence in the lives of those participating in this pursuit. If you pay close attention to what people say and engage their voice with thoughtful responses and critical curiosity, you'll not only help participants own the truth, but you'll model for them how they can think more critically.

CLOSING PRAYER

In these studies, we often (but not always) suggest you "close in prayer" at the end of the study. We're not telling you exactly how to pray or what to pray, but the idea is for you to "collect" your shared experience in a prayer focused on what your group learns about Jesus, or how he generously reveals himself through each session's particular pursuit. These prayers should be brief but "organic." In other words, simply talk to God about the impact of the study on the group members' lives—much the same way you'd talk to your best friend or spouse. If you're blank, simply thank God for who he is and what he's doing through the study.

WHAT TO CUT...AND NOT

Because of the learning approach we use in this series, you might need to cut part of a session because of time. That's OK, because coverage isn't the goal of these studies. Instead, focus on deeper learning and transformation. You can feel good about letting a conversation go on a little longer because it's going somewhere surprising and important. We've designed these studies to last an hour and 15 minutes from start to finish. We've taught this series several times, so we know you can get through the material in that time. We also know we've cut or abbreviated a few pieces along the way, just because a great conversation went longer than we planned or an unexpected catastrophe happened. One time, when we taught week 2, "Jesus Defines 'Good,' " our "taste expert" didn't show up. We gave participants a longer time to discuss a question while we put our heads together to decide what to do.

A few general guidelines about cutting stuff: Aim to cut from the middle of the session if you're tight on time, rather than the beginning or the end. Never cut an experience in favor of leader-talk. If you must choose between participants discovering a truth in discussion with others and you simply telling them the truth, opt for option A. Let others own what they're learning. You might be tempted to cut discussions short for the sake of time. If you do, you'll have a lot of frustrated people on your hands—people who simply don't have enough time to talk about the great question you asked them to pursue. These frustrated people then have a hurdle to overcome if they're going to return to the study the next week. So, cut and condense what you have to say in favor of retaining what others have to say. Don't worry, you'll still have many opportunities to guide, influence, and frame the discussions.

ANOTHER OPTION

You can also extend the series past 10 weeks. If you like the discussion and if people enter into new territory in their understanding of Jesus, feel free to camp out on a discussion or activity or exploration. You might want to split that session in two and finish the second half the following week. Remember, the goal isn't to cover the material, but to help people answer Jesus' great question: "Who do you say I am?"

That said, we've constructed the studies more like a good story than a bulleted list of truths. Each contains a beginning, middle, and end. So if you leave people hanging in the middle of the story too often, you'll end up frustrating them. Only you know your group. Just be wise and tread carefully if you decide to carry a session over to a second week.

Finally, we want to remind you that you're about to change the life trajectory of the people who participate in this pursuit. This really will happen. People will get closer to Jesus, and some of them will be changed by that experience forever. Thanks for having the courage and the determination to be a part of the nuclear moments that are about to take place. Along with the participants in the study, you'll not only end up worshipping Jesus at a deeper level, you'll also give people the opportunity to think critically, to own their own insights, to personally help others find the truth, and to open themselves to God's revelation. Nothing is more fulfilling than grabbing people's attention for the express purpose of directing their focus to Jesus. Your joint pursuit will be glorious—in every sense of the word.

THE PURSUIT OF JESUS WEB SITE

For supplies, resources, and video clips that are only available on the Web, we've created a special Web site just for this series. You'll find it at www.pursuitofjesus .com. There you can find resources and links you'll need for the study, plus updates and a way to interact with us if you have questions or comments. And to help you capture the spirit and dynamics of leading this study, we videotaped a session and put it on the site—just click and watch.

GETTING R.E.A.L.

Aren't acronyms cute? In a book I recently finished writing, I promised the next book I'd tackle would be called *The Bonfire of the Acronyms*.

R.E.A.L. is an acronym that represents Group Publishing's passion for partnering with God to plunge people into transforming learning experiences. The purpose of this little primer is simply to help you to "lean toward" these teaching values as far as you can. We understand you're already a talented, experienced presenter with your own value system. All we ask is that you look for ways to bend your values toward those we know will powerfully transform the lives of people who pursue Jesus with you. That's it. We so appreciate what you bring to the table—not just your talents as a leader, but, more important, your heart.

Group Publishing's R.E.A.L. acronym represents our passion for teaching that "sticks." During this series you'll have dozens of opportunities to bring growth and transformation in the lives of hungry people. We urge you to treat those encounters as holy and worthy of "extra mile" attention.

At Group, we value and appreciate entertaining presentations as much as the next person, but we're *passionate* about unforgettable, life-changing learning experiences. People can leave a presentation entertained but unchanged. Our mission is to partner with God to do what he loves best—bring transformation and freedom.

So consider this a down-and-dirty overview of what R.E.A.L. is all about.

R—RELATIONAL

This simply means people learn better, and retain more, when they learn in the context of a conversation instead of the context of a lecture. The easy way to accomplish this is to ask more questions of the people you lead and to get them talking to each other throughout your time together. When you get people into pairs or trios or groups at tables and you give them a great question to talk about—followed by feedback and debriefing—you help them own what they learn.

E—EXPERIENTIAL

Every learning researcher agrees that experiences have far more power to teach than the merely written or spoken word (Group Publishing's leaders, Thom and Joani Schultz, have written two books on it—*Why Nobody Learns Much of Anything at Church* and *The Dirt on Learning*). When you involve people in "direct" experiences within the context of your study, the chances that they'll never forget what you teach go way, way up.

A direct experience means involving people in something that engages all (or most) of their senses. This might mean building something or tearing something down. It might mean taking away one sense to heighten the experience of the remaining senses. It might mean asking participants to "practice" what you just "preached." In any case, the best direct experiences are simple, short, and memorable.

Over the years I've learned something from Joani Schultz about leading people into learning experiences: "If you believe they'll do it, they will." So, when you think about your teaching, tell yourself you *know* that your study participants will do whatever you tell them to do.

A—APPLICABLE

My least favorite (but often used) teaching strategy is when speakers pelt people with broad imperatives ("Your relationship with God depends on regular, consistent quiet times") divorced from the practical "hooks" that can help people take the first steps toward change and growth ("If quiet times seem daunting or even impossible to you, start out small by using a book such as *My Utmost for His Highest* by Oswald Chambers—each day's entry takes just a couple of minutes to read"). In this series, *you* are the bridge between "what-why" and "how."

If you tell participants to do something, you should have a practical illustration, personal story, or accessible task to hook to it so they have light on the path you urge them to take.

L—LEARNER-BASED

The learner—not the leader or teacher—is the true judge of how much learning and growth takes place. This means the goal isn't just delivering the material you prepare and calling it good. Rather, the goal is to slow down, simplify, and engage.

How will you know for sure that the people you present to "get it"? Well, by the time you're ready to lead a session, you already "own" your material—you're inside of it so much that it's part of your belief system. What will it take to lead participants into the same kind of "ownership" relationship with this series?

The activities in these studies help you release people to teach each other what you hope they'll learn. The idea is that as participants learn something, they quickly transition into teaching someone else what they've learned.

By the way, if you need more ammo on the importance of teaching in R.E.A.L. ways, remember that this acronym represents Jesus' teaching approach. He asked almost 300 questions in the gospels, and spent a lot of time just hanging out and talking with people. He often led his followers into experiences that he then helped them debrief. He made his teaching applicable by using stories and examples that resonated with the everyday life experiences of his followers. And he always followed up with people, checking to see if they "got" what he taught.

So, go forth and teach like Jesus!

IN PURSUIT OF JESUS

WEEK 1: WHO DO YOU SAY I AM?

PRIOR TO THIS SESSION

▶ Set up a computer to play or project the video parody "Ron Burgundy Interviews Jesus" from the link on the In Pursuit of Jesus Web site (www.pursuit ofjesus.com). Or you can find the video on YouTube.com by going to the site and typing "Ron Burgundy interviews Jesus" in the search box.

▶ Set up a boombox or stereo system to play music.

▶ Set up a white board or big pad of paper, along with markers.

▶ Cue up track 11, "Oh, Lord, You're Beautiful," on Keith Green's *The Ministry Years Vol. 2: 1980-1982* CD for your closing worship. (You can also find this song on Green's compilation album *Oh Lord, You're Beautiful* and on his original album, *So You Wanna Go Back to Egypt*.)

WELCOME AND INTRODUCTION (20 MINUTES)

After you welcome people, tell a little about why you've decided to do this series. What drew you to it? Why is it important to you? Talk a bit about how your relationship with Jesus has grown through the years. Remind your class or group to read the short introduction to the study in their participant books sometime after today's study. That will help them prepare for the pursuit you're about to take together.

Then say something like:

> In this 10-week pursuit, we'll be diving into a central, riveting question Jesus asked his disciples and now asks us: "Who do you say I am?" Jesus asked his disciples this question just after he'd fed the

5,000 with a few loaves and fishes. When it was evening and time for everyone to return home, Jesus gathered the disciples away from the crowds to debrief the experience with them.

First, Jesus asked them what people were saying about him. He wanted to know who they said he was. The disciples told him that, basically, the people thought he was a prophet. Then Jesus got more personal. He asked the disciples, "Who do you say I am?" Peter answered this question, "The Christ of God."

Even if we've read this story before, maybe we haven't paid much attention to the way we'd answer Jesus' question. It's such a basic question—maybe we think we know everything we need to know about Jesus. But in our complacency about this question, we've missed who Jesus really is.

In fact, when it comes to our views on Jesus, we might have more in common with fictional newscaster Ron Burgundy than we'd like to believe. This is Ron Burgundy, played by comedian Will Ferrell, doing an interview with Jim Caviezel as a goofy opening to the 2004 MTV Movie Awards. Jim Caviezel played Jesus in Mel Gibson's *The Passion of the Christ*. Let's watch...

SHOW VIDEO CLIP

Show the clip from the MTV Movie Awards, where Ron Burgundy interviews "Jesus." After the clip, *say something like:*

Is it too much of a stretch to say that many followers of Christ function a lot like Ron Burgundy in this clip? Obviously, we don't act like a doofus with Jesus. But toss out some answers here—what did you see in this interview that revealed common beliefs about Jesus?

THE RULES OF ENGAGEMENT

Whenever you gather input from the whole group—either from a question you ask or as they report back on discussions they have—use these tips to remember how to prime the discussion, ask follow-up questions, and engage the responses you get back:

1. Embrace every answer. Write a condensed version of each one on your white board or pad.

2. If an answer seems vague, confusing, wrong, or sounds like the Sunday school "right" answer, follow up with one of these go-deeper comments or questions:
   - ▶ "Please say more about what you mean."
   - ▶ "I've never thought of that before—could you explain more?"
   - ▶ "That seems to contradict what we commonly believe—could you be more specific?"
   - ▶ "That's the answer we expect. How would you explain that to someone who doesn't know the 'expected' answer?"

3. If an answer is surprising or insightful, ask the person to say a little more (unless the answer was detailed in the first place). You can ask others in the group to expand on that answer, too.

4. When someone specifically connects with where the study is headed, highlight that answer as important to pay attention to.

5. Aim for developing an atmosphere that resembles a good conversation, where you and other group members interact all the time with what someone says.

After you gather responses from the group, *say something like:*

Sometimes, we act a lot like Ron Burgundy. We don't know Jesus all that well, but we think we do. We relate to Jesus like he's a magician or a celebrity or some kind of mythical figure.

Honestly, we're not unlike Jesus' original disciples. They often had a hard time understanding who Jesus really is, even though they hung

out with him and experienced so much. Jesus often said something like "You still don't understand me" to his disciples.

For example, listen to this story about Thomas and Philip and Jesus, from John 14:4-9:

" 'You know the way to the place where I am going.' Thomas said to him, 'Lord, we don't know where you are going, so how can we know the way?' Jesus answered, 'I am the way and the truth and the life. No one comes to the Father except through me. If you really knew me, you would know my Father as well. From now on, you do know him and have seen him.' Philip said, 'Lord, show us the Father and that will be enough for us.' Jesus answered: 'Don't you know me, Philip, even after I have been among you such a long time? Anyone who has seen me has seen the Father.' "

Ask the group something like:

Are the disciples stupid or thick or slow or...what? Why do they have such a hard time understanding Jesus?

After you have a few responses, *say something like:*

In a way, we're all like Philip. We've spent a lot of time with Jesus, but we don't seem to *get* him very well. We go through life trying to build a relationship with a Jesus we only think we know. In this series, we'll take Jesus' big question—Who do you say I am?—as a big, plump challenge. We'll explore the answer in ways that might be a little different for you—through discussions, film clips, music, experiences, art, and group interactions.

HOW WELL DO WE REALLY KNOW JESUS?
(20 MINUTES)

On your white board or pad, write: "95/45/10." *Then say something like:*

> Let's explore some thoughts that get at the foundation of our belief
> about Jesus. Researchers at the University of North Carolina have
> found that 95 percent of Americans believe in God, 45 percent of
> Americans go to church, but only 10 percent have a "devoted faith."[1]
> Researchers say the 10 percent with a "devoted faith" are people
> for whom faith in Christ is the central hub of their life. Everything
> revolves around their faith. Their relationship with Jesus filters into
> their everyday life in both regular and profound ways.

Ask something like:

> For the 95 percent-ers—or even the 45 percent-ers—why isn't
> Jesus the central focus of their lives? What accounts for this 95-45-10
> progression in our culture? Let's hear some reasons…

Remember to use The Rules of Engagement. After you collect participants' responses,
say something like:

> Could it be that Jesus is mildly attractive to us, and we even study
> about him, but he doesn't *really* capture our hearts?
> Listen to this quote from *Wild at Heart* by author John Eldredge:
> "I am convinced beyond a doubt of this: God wants to be loved. He
> wants to be a priority to someone. How could we have missed this?
> From cover to cover, from beginning to end, the cry of God's heart
> is, 'Why won't you choose me?' It is amazing to me how humble, how

vulnerable God is on this point. 'You will…find me,' says the Lord, 'when you seek me with all your heart' (Jer. 29:13). In other words, 'Look for me, pursue me—I want you to pursue me.' Amazing. As Tozer says, 'God waits to be wanted.' "[2]

Even though God invites us into intimacy, our everyday lives often funnel our passions into other pursuits—relationships, career, family. Whatever captures our passions has the power to shape us. Mimi Wilson, a Bible teacher, speaker, and author, says, "We'll be shaped by who we think God is—that's why God told us not to worship idols."[3] Isn't that profound? And true?

In my life, sometimes I've thought that Jesus was *(share a personal example of one way you've had a limited or even incorrect impression of Jesus—for example, that he's primarily a nice guy or a distant rule-giver)*, **and the result in my life has been** *(share how that limited impression of Jesus actually affected your life—for example, you glossed over the stories of Jesus acting not-so-nice in Scripture, or you've had a hard time understanding the concept of grace)*.

Ask something like:

In your booklet, write some words that describe the way you see Jesus. Don't write canned phrases from the Bible or other words you think you should write. Instead, be brutally honest with yourself. How do you *really* experience Jesus, and what do you *really* think of him?

After a couple of minutes, have participants get with one other person to form a pair (if your group includes spouses, remember to separate them).

Say something like:

Now I want you to think about your list of descriptive words. Think about one way you've been shaped by the way you see Jesus—

a part of who you are that directly connects to a word or phrase you listed. Then share that with your partner. For example, if you've always seen Jesus as a "nice guy," maybe you feel uncomfortable with "harder" stories about him—like the time he cleared the Temple with a whip. OK? Go!

After five minutes or so, get the group's attention, and ask a few people to tell about their partner discussions. Remember to follow The Rules of Engagement.

GETTING CLOSER TO JESUS (25 MINUTES)

After the feedback time, *say something like:*

Tom Melton, an author, speaker, and pastor of a Denver church, often says:

"We don't *really* believe Jesus is beautiful, because we wouldn't describe our relationship with him as so much work if we did."[4]

This is a great example of how our view of Jesus shapes our relationship with him. Maybe we "work" at our relationship with Jesus because we make faith a big "supposed to" in our lives. What if, instead, we tasted more deeply of Jesus' beauty? How would that affect the way we describe our relationship with him?

In this pursuit, we'll find out. We'll use our heads *and* our hearts to approach him. Psalm 27:4 says: "One thing I ask of the Lord, this is what I seek: that I may dwell in the house of the Lord all the days of my life, to gaze upon the beauty of the Lord and to seek him in his temple." "Gaze upon his beauty" is another way of saying we'll pursue God through the beauty of Jesus' life and words. But to do that we have to get closer to him.

Make sure each person has something to write on (the booklet) and something to write with. Divide the group in half, and tell half the people to stand at one end of your meeting area and the other half to stand at the other end. Instruct each person to choose someone from the other side of the room and to stand directly across from that person.

This is a good place to tell participants that during this study series you'll be asking them to plunge into experiences without the normal critical ways we try to resist doing new things. Remember, you can ask them to simply "play with" what you ask them to do—to simply jump in and do it. As people follow your instructions, write "the true progression" paragraph (on page 37) on your white board or pad.

Say something like:

Take two minutes to write as many descriptive words as you can about the person at the other end of the room. Challenge yourself! Use any descriptive words you want, including impressions you have of that person. By the way, no talking during this experience. (You may have to remind them of this rule.)

After two minutes, instruct partners to move very close to each other, within six inches of each other's faces. *Then say something like:*

I know this invades your space a little, but just keep playing with me and pretend it's OK to be so close. Now take another two minutes to write descriptive words you missed before. Remember, no talking…

After two minutes, tell everyone to return to their seats. Have them look at their lists, *then ask these questions, one at a time, and write their answers on your white board:*

▶ **What changed in your descriptive words when you got closer?**
▶ **What's something you liked and didn't like about getting closer?**
▶ **How might getting closer to Jesus change your perspective of him?**
▶ **What's good about getting closer to Jesus, and what's hard about getting closer to him?**

Remember to use the Rules of Engagement as you lead people into this debriefing time. After 10 minutes or so, close the debriefing time by *saying something like:*

Here is the true progression that marks our life with Christ (you should have written this on your white board or pad as people participated in the "closer" experience):

Get to know Jesus well, because the more you know him, the more you'll love him, and the more you love him, the more you'll want to follow him, and the more you follow him, the more you'll become like him, and the more you become like him, the more you become yourself.

I love the last line—"the more you become yourself."
Ask something like:

▶ **What do you think that last line means?**

After a few responses, *say something like:*

Sometimes we read the Bible like a fairy tale rather than a life story. We treat the stories of Jesus in the Bible kind of like we do nursery rhymes. We know they contain truths, but we don't think of the characters as really real. Sometimes we look to the Bible for formulas and patterns and ways to exert control over our messy lives. But what if the whole of the Bible was really an invitation to experience Jesus' beauty? And what if the Bible's stories about Jesus were intended to draw us to him—to bring us closer to intimacy with him? And what if, as we grow more intimate with him, we discover the person inside he's always intended us to be?

Ask people to close their eyes and get comfortable. Then take them back to the hillside near Bethsaida, where Jesus fed the 5,000 with five loaves of bread and two fish

(Luke 9:12-20). The passage ends with Jesus' great question: "Who do you say I am?" The idea is to place the people in your class into the story as a character. Use the script titled "The Big Question" on page 39, or just use the script as a template to create your own version. Most important, take time to tell about details—smells, sounds, facial expressions—information that will help people feel a part of the story.

When you finish telling the story, ask participants to keep their eyes closed for a closing song.

CLOSING WORSHIP (10 MINUTES)

Play the song "Oh Lord, You're Beautiful" by Keith Green. Ask people to close their eyes and listen.

When the song is over, ask people to keep their eyes closed as you *say (softly) something like*:

> **Deep in our hearts, we long to taste more of Jesus, to know him better just because we feel so drawn to him. In this study, we'll taste more of Jesus by continually answering the greatest question ever asked: "Who do you say I am?" We'll try to taste the beauty of the mystery of God, as revealed in his Son, Jesus.**

Softly read aloud this John Eldredge quote from his book *Captivating* (written with his wife, Stasi):

> **"God yearns to be known. But he wants to be *sought after* by those who would know him. He says, 'You will seek me and find me when you seek me with all your heart' (Jer. 29:13). There is dignity here; God does not throw himself at any passerby. He is no harlot. If you would know him you must love him; you must seek him with your whole heart."[5]**

Close with a short prayer. Prayer is conversation, so simply talk to Jesus about the experience you just walked through. This is a great place to thank him for

- ▶ pursuing us with questions that draw us to him.
- ▶ pursuing us first, enabling us to pursue him.

THE BIG QUESTION

Luke 9:12-20

(Don't go through this story too quickly. Take time to pause, to add emotion, and to add emphasis to the story. As you lead people back to the time of Jesus, don't be afraid to add details that come to you.)

Imagine you're a Jew living at the time of Jesus. You live in your hometown of Bethsaida, the fishing village near the shore of the Sea of Galilee where your friends Andrew, Peter, and Phillip were born. Through them, you hear about a man named Jesus—they call him a rabbi. You've even heard whispers that he might be the Messiah. Jesus is coming to Bethsaida to teach, and the word spreads like a wildfire through the surrounding country.

You and thousands of others make your way to a hill just outside of town. As Jesus and his disciples arrive, you jostle in the sea of people to get a better look at him. It's hot, and the smell of the throng and the dust in the air overpower your senses.

Jesus sits down and begins to describe what he calls the "kingdom of God." He teaches with a simple assurance—a relaxed urgency. Later, the friends of the sick and the lame push past you, helping their needy friends to the feet of Jesus. They come in droves! And you're startled—no, you're shocked—as you watch Jesus touch these people, then see them walk away healed. A buzz of electricity fills the air—a palpable sense of awe and expectation like you've never experienced before.

By now, the sun hangs low in the sky and the heat slowly gives way to the cool of the evening. Your hunger hits the pit of your stomach. Like those around you, you don't want to leave. But you're also hungry and wondering where you'll get food. You see someone hand Jesus a basket with some bread and fish in it. And you think, *well at least Jesus and his disciples will get something to eat.*

But then Jesus looks up, blesses the food, and asks his disciples to serve it to the gathered thousands. You look at the people on either side of you, and they glance back with the same look of curiosity and skepticism. When the food makes it to where you're seated, you see plenty still remains for you to take. The more people take, the more there is!

The astonishment of what you've seen so far washes over you. As people finish eating, you see Jesus and his disciples slipping away, around the back of the hill. The crowds turn to go home, but something rivets you. You feel awkward and self-conscious, yet you feel drawn to Jesus like a magnet. So you casually follow him as he retreats. You think you won't be noticed because you carefully act as though you're just wandering in the same direction.

You round the top of the hill and see Jesus sitting with his disciples. In fact, you're startled to find them sitting so close. You plop down right there to listen. You hear Jesus ask his friends something like "Who do those people say that I am?" As he asks the question, he glances over at you—you realize he sees you, and you start to stand up to leave. But he has a smile on his face—a little grin, really. So you settle back on the ground and stay.

You hear his disciples answer his question by saying, "John the Baptist...Elijah...or one of the very old prophets." After a pause, you see Jesus scan the faces of his disciples with that same grin. He glances up at you, and is still locked on your eyes when he asks, "But what about you—who do you say I am?" He lowers his gaze again to look at his disciples. You feel something burning in the back of your throat....You hear Peter say, "The Christ of God." Then you see the look on Jesus' face change as he warns them to keep that to themselves...for now.

Then, for the last time, he glances back at you. The grin is gone, replaced with something like a look of invitation...

ENDNOTE 1: The National Study of Youth and Religion report: *Soul Searching: The Religious and Spiritual Lives of American Teenagers,* by Christian Smith and Melinda Lundquist Denton (Oxford University Press, 2005).
ENDNOTE 2: John Eldredge, *Wild at Heart* (Thomas Nelson Publishers, 2001), p. 36.
ENDNOTE 3: From an unpublished lecture by Mimi Wilson.
ENDNOTE 4: From an unpublished sermon by Tom Melton, pastor of Greenwood Community Church in Denver.
ENDNOTE 5: John and Stasi Eldredge, *Captivating: Unveiling the Mystery of a Woman's Soul* (Thomas Nelson Publishers, 2005), p. 41.

WEEK 2: JESUS DEFINES "GOOD"

PRIOR TO THIS SESSION

▶ Set out two sets of cups—equal numbers of each. The cups in the first set should each contain a dab of A-1 steak sauce, and the cups in the second set should each hold a dab of Heinz 57 steak sauce. You'll be giving participants a cup of each kind of steak sauce, so you need enough to give a set of two cups to each person.

▶ Invite a chef or accomplished cook from your congregation to join this session. When the person shows up, don't point out that he or she is a chef. You want a person with a well-developed palate to participate in this session's taste-test— to compare the flavors an accomplished gourmet can discern to those a normal person can discern. Before the study, tell the chef that you'll be asking group members to list flavors they can discern by tasting steak sauce—ask him or her to refrain from revealing his or her list until you ask for it. *Option:* If it's not possible to get a chef or cook to attend, use the list of "Steak-Sauce Flavors" cheat sheet included with this session instead.

▶ Set up a computer to play or project one of the Jesus Parody videos created by Vintage21 church in North Carolina—our favorite is #3, where Jesus speaks to each of his disciples on a hillside. You can access the clip from our Web site (www.pursuitofjesus.com). Or go to the Vintage21 Web site (www.vintage21 .com). Just roll your cursor over the "Sunday" link; you'll see the link "Video"— click on it and you'll find the four videos listed. You can also download the videos from Google Videos by going to Google, then clicking on the video link, then searching for Vintage21—just download Jesus Video #3. The videos also have their own MySpace page at www.myspace.com/vintage21jesusvideos.

▶ Set up a boombox or stereo system, ready to play music.

▶ Set up a white board or big pad of paper, along with markers.

▶ Cue up track 3, "How Great Is Our God," on Chris Tomlin's *Arriving* CD for your closing worship.

▶ *Optional:* Buy a doughnut for each participant to serve at the start of the session.

WELCOME AND INTRODUCTION (15 MINUTES)

If you have doughnuts or another tasty treat, after you welcome people, ask everyone to taste their treat. *Then ask something like:*

▶ **What makes a doughnut** [or your substitute] **taste so good?**

▶ **Do people generally agree on what tastes good and what doesn't?**

▶ **How do we know when something tastes good to us and when it doesn't?**

After the group discusses the questions, *say something like:*

In this study we'll learn what it's like to taste more deeply of Jesus and discover how he defines "good." Remember, instead of looking for principles in the life of Jesus that will help us live our lives, we want to focus on the person of Jesus—to get as close to him as we can. When you get close to Jesus, transformation happens naturally—like fruit growing on a healthy tree. We want to answer his big question: "Who do you say I am?"

In 1 Corinthians 2:1-2, the Apostle Paul said that he was determined to know nothing but Jesus. In fact, here's the whole context of what he said: "And when I came to you, brethren, I did not come with superiority of speech or of wisdom, proclaiming to you the testimony of God. For I determined to know nothing among you except Jesus Christ, and Him crucified" (NAS).

We want our class to have tunnel vision. We could talk about and pursue a lot of different things. But we'll continually bring the focus back to Paul's determination to know nothing "except Jesus Christ, and Him crucified."

THE RULES OF ENGAGEMENT

Whenever you gather input from the whole group—either from a question you ask or as they report back on discussions they have—use these tips to remember how to prime the discussion, ask follow-up questions, and engage the responses you get back:

1. Embrace every answer. Write a condensed version of each one on your white board or pad.

2. If an answer seems vague, confusing, wrong, or sounds like the Sunday school "right" answer, follow up with one of these go-deeper comments or questions:
   - ▶ "Please say more about what you mean."
   - ▶ "I've never thought of that before—could you explain more?"
   - ▶ "That seems to contradict what we commonly believe—could you be more specific?"
   - ▶ "That's the answer we expect. How would you explain that to someone who doesn't know the 'expected' answer?"

3. If an answer is surprising or insightful, ask the person to say a little more (unless the answer was detailed in the first place). You can ask others in the group to expand on that answer, too.

4. When someone specifically connects with where the study is headed, highlight that answer as important to pay attention to.

5. Aim for developing an atmosphere that resembles a good conversation, where you and other group members interact all the time with what someone says.

Let's stick with the assumption that we *really don't know* what we think we know about Jesus. That's exactly what the Vintage21 Church in North Carolina did when they decided to spend a whole month pursuing the "real" Jesus. They took a really old film about Jesus, extracted four scenes, and then put their own soundtrack with the scenes. Let's watch one of those scenes together.

SHOW VIDEO CLIP

Show the Jesus Parody #3 video clip—the one where Jesus talks to his disciples on a hillside—created by the Vintage21 church in North Carolina.

After the clip, *ask something like:*

> ▶ **What misconceptions about Jesus does this little clip poke fun at?**

Get a few responses, and remember to use The Rules of Engagement.

Then say something like:

> **Remember how quickly Peter responded when Jesus asked: "Who do you say I am?" He gave the right answer, but then he quickly showed he didn't really understand his own definition.**
>
> **In Matthew's version of this encounter, soon after Peter's "You are the Christ" response, he tells Jesus that he'll never allow him to be harmed. Peter didn't really understand what Jesus came to do, so Jesus says to Peter, "Get behind me, Satan!" Peter knew the right answer—and that was good—but he didn't really understand who Jesus was. Let's approach knowing Jesus with a different mindset—a mindset that's awake, thinking, detailed, curious, and open.**

JESUS DEFINES GOOD (30 MINUTES)

Tell participants to take just two minutes to list in their booklets as many things as they can think of that are "good." They should think about what they'd classify as fundamentally good. Their list might include anything (such as ice cream or nature or music). It doesn't have to be "spiritual." After two minutes, have people pair up with a partner (remember to separate spouses).

Say something like:

> **Share your list, and then talk about how you decide what's good and what's not. What's your criteria for "good"?**

After a few minutes of discussion, ask people to simply tell you their criteria for "good." List everything they say on your white board or pad. Remember to follow The Rules of Engagement.

Then *ask these follow-up questions:*

> ▶ **Is the way we define "good" universal or does it vary by situation?**
> ▶ **Are any of our criteria universal? What exceptions do you see?**
> ▶ **How do we really know what's good and what's not?**

After five minutes or so of discussion, *say something like:*

> **When we closely examine our definitions of "good," we start to discover how inherently "crumbly" they are. Jesus thought this question of defining good was crucial.**

Read aloud Luke 18:18-23:

> **"A certain ruler asked him, 'Good teacher, what must I do to inherit eternal life?' 'Why do you call me good?' Jesus answered. 'No one is good—except God alone. You know the commandments: "Do not commit adultery, do not murder, do not steal, do not give false testimony, honor your father and mother." ' 'All these I have kept since I was a boy,' he said. When Jesus heard this, he said to him, 'You still lack one thing. Sell everything you have and give to the poor, and you will have treasure in heaven. Then come, follow me.' When he heard this, he became very sad, because he was a man of great wealth."**

Now say something like:

> **Before Jesus answered the young man's question, he stopped to target something first—the man's casual use of the word "good."**

Jesus wants to make the point that only God is good.

Ask something like:

▶ **Why did Jesus respond the way he did with this young man?**
▶ **Why did Jesus tell him to sell everything he had and follow him?**

Remember to use The Rules of Engagement.
After a few minutes of discussion, *say something like:*

Could it be that Jesus asked the young man to disconnect from his own "false goodness" so he could connect to the true goodness of God? In John 15:5 Jesus says, "I am the vine; you are the branches." Our life, our goodness, is tied to Jesus. Without him we have no life, no goodness. According to Jesus, only he is good.
So let's explore how we can know Jesus' goodness more deeply. Let's use Psalm 34:8 as our guide: "Taste and see that the Lord is good."

Give each person two cups with a different steak sauce in each cup. Tell participants that their mission is answering the questions under "A Taste Test" on page 23 in their booklets. Ask them to answer the question for one steak sauce first and then the other. Give them two minutes or so for each steak sauce, and let them know when they should switch to the second one. Read the question they're answering:

List every single taste you can discern in each sauce. For example, if you wanted to make this yourself without a recipe, what would you include?

After the participants have made their own lists, ask them to shout out flavors from the first steak sauce. List on your white board or pad every flavor people discerned. Then do the same for the other steak sauce.
After the group shares, ask the invited chef or cook to share his or her list of flavors. The idea is that this person will have a more extensive list because of a more tuned

palate. (If you can't find a chef or cook to attend the session, use the list of steak-sauce flavors included on page 50 as a comparison instead.)

Ask something like:

> ▶ **Why is the chef's list longer than our combined list?**

After a few responses, *say something like:*

The chef's list drills down into the nuances, the details, the essence of the tastes. A chef can list more flavors because his or her tasting ability is better trained.

When your palate can discern more flavors, you enjoy food even more. Each meal becomes a real feast. A gourmet can appreciate the essence of food.

We want to be gourmets when it comes to Jesus. We want to appreciate the essence of Jesus.

Ask the chef something like:

> ▶ **What would an untrained person need to do to better develop the ability to taste well?** *(Write answers on white board or pad.)*
>
> *Then ask everyone something like:*

> ▶ **What connections can we make from improving our palate to improving our ability to taste Jesus well?** *(Write answers on white board or pad.)*

If no one else cites these connections, add them to your list and talk about them briefly:

> ▶ Slow down
> ▶ Become aware
> ▶ Pay attention
> ▶ Taste often

A DEEPER TASTE OF JESUS (20 MINUTES)

Say something like:

> Remember, Psalm 34:8 says: "Taste and see that the Lord is good."
> Let's implement what we just discussed. Let's do a little "Taste-Test
> Challenge" to savor the good in Jesus. Then we'll let that taste define
> what is good.

Have people get back with their partners from the "Jesus Defines Good" section from earlier in the session. Assign one of the following stories to each pair (if you have more pairs than stories, give the same story to more than one pair; if you have fewer pairs than stories, assign fewer stories). Tell partners they'll have five or six minutes to discuss the following question:

> ▶ **What did Jesus do that was good? List as many things as you can in your booklet.**

Assign these passages to pairs (make sure pairs have at least one Bible between them):
> ▶ Luke 4:1-13: Jesus tempted by the devil
> ▶ Luke 5:27-32: Jesus calls Matthew (called Levi before he became a disciple), parties with tax collectors
> ▶ Luke 6:6-11: Jesus heals man's withered hand on Sabbath
> ▶ Luke 8:26-39: Jesus casts demons out of Gerasene demoniac
> ▶ Luke 12:1-12: Jesus gives warnings and encouragements
> ▶ Luke 14:16-24: Parable of the dinner

After five or six minutes, have pairs report on their discussion, asking them to very briefly describe their stories. Remember to follow The Rules of Engagement. *Ask additional questions such as:*

> ▶ **Why do these words and actions represent "good"?**
> ▶ **What's surprising about the "goodness" of Jesus' words and actions?**
> ▶ **What can you pick out about what Jesus likes and doesn't like from these stories?**

To close the discussion, *say something like:*

> If only Jesus is good, then his likes and dislikes, his definitions for what's good and what's not, should be train tracks that help us arrive at our own definition of good.

CLOSING RESPONSE AND WORSHIP (10 MINUTES)

Remind your group again about Jesus' question that you're trying to answer: "Who do you say I am?" Direct participants into a closing time of worship by asking them to close their eyes, *then say something like:*

> Think about how God is bigger to you than when you walked into this room. In the quiet, think of the words that remind you of how you tasted God today—how is Jesus good? Write those words in your booklet if you'd like.

After a couple of minutes, play "How Great Is Our God" by Chris Tomlin, from the album *Arriving*. Ask people to simply close their eyes as they listen. In later studies you and the study participants will look at the song summaries or actual lyrics to songs as you listen, but for this one you can just close your eyes.

Then close in prayer. With everyone's eyes closed, invite participants to speak out one word that represents something great about God. You might ask them to finish the sentence "God, you are…" Then end the prayer by repeating back to God some of the words people speak, including your own.

STEAK-SAUCE FLAVORS

A Cheat Sheet

Use this list of flavors from both steak sauces if you can't get a chef to attend your session. This list was developed with input from a "master chef" who tasted each steak sauce and identified the flavors he found. Since the makers of each steak sauce keep a portion of their "recipe" secret, the list of flavors is open to interpretation. Your own "expert taster" might find something the chef who developed this list didn't. That's great!

Heinz 57	A-1
Tomato	Tomato
Sugar	Citrus/Orange Peel
Malt Vinegar	Worcestershire
Mustard	Sugar
White Pepper	Vinegar
Tumeric	Onion
Honey	Garlic
Garlic	Clove
Onion	Cardamom
Raisin	Salt
Apple	White Pepper
	Coriander
	Raisin

IN PURSUIT OF JESUS

WEEK 3: JESUS AND HIS PARABLES

PRIOR TO THIS SESSION

- ▶ Set up a boombox or stereo system to play music.
- ▶ Set up a white board or big pad of paper, along with markers.
- ▶ Cue up track 11, "Grace," on U2's *All That You Can't Leave Behind* CD for your opening worship.
- ▶ Set out Rich Mullins' *The World as Best as I Remember It Vol. 1* CD for your closing worship. You'll play track 1, "Step By Step," at that time.

WELCOME AND INTRODUCTION (30 MINUTES)

When people arrive welcome them. Then ask them to get comfortable, close their eyes, and listen to the song "Grace" by U2 (a song summary is printed on page 61, or you can go to www.pursuitofjesus.com for a link to the actual lyrics online).

After the song, *say something like:*

Whether or not you recognized it, we opened with a kind of parable—a simple story that has both a surface meaning and a deeper meaning. The song is called "Grace" by U2.

In this session we're going to dive into the parables of Jesus. We want to go beyond just discovering their meaning to understanding why Jesus told so many of these stories.

Now take a couple of minutes to ask God to bring to mind *a story*— a specific story—that provides a good example of what it was like to grow up in your home as a child. For example, maybe the story of a specific family vacation would tell a stranger everything he needed to know about your family. Don't work too hard on this. Once a story surfaces, write a few words or sentences in your booklet to describe the story.

After a couple of minutes, *say something like:*

> Now take a few minutes to ask God to bring to mind *a story*—a specific story—that captures the essence of either your father or mother. For example, what did your father do every day when he came home from work? Write a few words or sentences in your booklet to describe this story.

After a couple of minutes, instruct people to each find a partner (remember to split up spouses). Have partners share both stories—about growing up in their families, and about one of their parents. Have one partner tell both stories first, then switch. Tell them that if one finishes before you say time is up, the partner should ask more follow-up questions by paying attention to gaps in the story or unexplained statements. Tell them to be curious, to not give up after the partner seems finished. And you'll let everyone know when it's time to switch partners.

After three minutes or so, tell partners to switch. Again, urge them to fill the time really digging after details in the stories.

After another three minutes or so, get their attention again. Ask for a volunteer to share his or her two stories with the whole group. Then pursue that person's story by asking questions that illuminate the value system, habits, practices, priorities, and driving force of the person's family. For example, you could *ask these questions (you don't need to ask all of these):*

▶ **What values were very important to your family?**
▶ **How did you see those values lived out in your family?**
▶ **Looking back at the way your parents made choices with time, what was most important to them?**

- ▶ How did the values your parents expressed agree or disagree with their actual life choices?
- ▶ How did your parents express love in your home? Was it generally conditional or unconditional? Why would you say that?

Then say something like:

Just as you told stories about your home and about a parent, Jesus also told stories about his Father and about life in his family. These stories are called parables. Jesus told 55 parables—they make up a large percentage of his "teaching." If you collect all the parables together, almost all of them answer one (or both) of these questions:

- ▶ Who is God?
- ▶ What is life like in God's kingdom (his *home*)?

Jesus' Father's name is Yahweh. His "home" is called the kingdom of God. The Trinity—Father, Son, and Holy Spirit—existed before everything. They had—and still have—a life together. They have their own community. They live passionately with one another according to a deeply entrenched value system. And you might remember from our last study that everything about their value system is "good."

In the Old Testament, God repeatedly urges his people to "walk in my ways." But he also says: "For my thoughts are not your thoughts, neither are your ways my ways" (Isaiah 55:8).

Ask something like:

- ▶ What are "the ways" of God?

After a few responses, *add the following insights if no one has mentioned them:*

- ▶ God's first shot at teaching us his ways, his value system, was basically the law and the prophets in the Old Testament. The Ten Commandments provide a great example of God's value system.
- ▶ God's second shot at teaching us his ways was, essentially, through his Son, Jesus.

Then say something like:

Even though God took great pains to share his family value system with us, these values sometimes seem like customs from a foreign culture. For example, ever wonder why instead of shaking hands in many cultures, people bow to each other? Well, in India, a jug and the left palm take the place of toilet paper, while in Indonesia, one might grow a long fingernail on the left hand for this purpose. As Americans, we have a hard time understanding these customs. We need an explanation!

(If you'd rather highlight an alternate custom, choose one from "Strange Customs" on page 62.)

Sometimes the customs and traditions and practices of God's family also seem foreign to us. Remember, original sin kicked Adam and Eve—and all of humanity to this day—out of the garden, our intended home with God. So Jesus must translate the personality and practices of his Father and the nature of life in God's kingdom into something we can understand—something that gives us a flavor of the mystery that represents his personality and kingdom. So Jesus told stories or parables.

Read aloud Matthew 13:10-13:

"The disciples came to him and asked, 'Why do you speak to the people in parables?' He replied, 'The knowledge of the secrets of the

kingdom of heaven has been given to you, but not to them. Whoever
has will be given more, and he will have an abundance. Whoever does
not have, even what he has will be taken from him. This is why I speak
to them in parables: Though seeing, they do not see; though hearing,
they do not hear or understand.' "

Ask something like:

> ▶ **What did Jesus mean by this explanation of why he spoke in
> parables?**

After you gather many responses, add to the discussion by sharing the following
insights (if no one has already mentioned them):

> **Jesus seems to be "planting" parables, like seeds, so that insights
> into God's character and kingdom slowly grow in people. Maybe those
> seeds stay in the soil of our souls until they're watered and fertilized
> and poke through into the light of our understanding. We all need the
> special help of parables to understand a God who is more glorious and
> beautiful than our natural understanding can comprehend.**

THE KINGDOM OF GOD IS LIKE... (15 MINUTES)

parables

Form trios and launch them into a deeper discovery of the value system and customs of
God's family. Assign each trio one of the parables from the "Kingdom of God" list in
their booklet (they're also in this leaders guide on page 64). Instruct trios to read their
assigned parable and list as many truths as they can about the values, practices, and priorities of the kingdom of God.

> ▶ Parable of Wheat and Weeds—Matthew 13:24-30: God is more concerned
> about growing wheat than pulling weeds.
> ▶ Parable of the Pine Nut—Matthew 13:31-32: What seems small can grow
> huge. Strength is nurtured over time.

- Parable of the Yeast—Matthew 13:33: A small addition makes a big difference.
- Parable of the Treasure in the Field—Matthew 13:44: Treasure belongs to those who appreciate it.
- Parable of the Pearl of Great Price—Matthew 13:45-46: Good things come to those who know treasure when they see it.
- Parable of the Big Fishnet—Matthew 13:47-50: The redeemed and unredeemed are allowed to grow together. It's not obvious which is good and bad.

THE RULES OF ENGAGEMENT

Whenever you gather input from the whole group—either from a question you ask or as they report back on discussions they have—use these tips to remember how to prime the discussion, ask follow-up questions, and engage the responses you get back:

1. Embrace every answer. Write a condensed version of each one on your white board or pad.
2. If an answer seems vague, confusing, wrong, or sounds like the Sunday school "right" answer, follow up with one of these go-deeper comments or questions:
   - "Please say more about what you mean."
   - "I've never thought of that before—could you explain more?"
   - "That seems to contradict what we commonly believe—could you be more specific?"
   - "That's the answer we expect. How would you explain that to someone who doesn't know the 'expected' answer?"
3. If an answer is surprising or insightful, ask the person to say a little more (unless the answer was detailed in the first place). You can ask others in the group to expand on that answer, too.
4. When someone specifically connects with where the study is headed, highlight that answer as important to pay attention to.
5. Aim for developing an atmosphere that resembles a good conversation, where you and other group members interact all the time with what someone says.

After five minutes or so, ask a spokesperson from each trio to tell about the parable they studied, and what truths their trio gleaned about Jesus' home, the kingdom of God. Remember to follow The Rules of Engagement.

After you hear from each group, *say something like:*

What happens when we more deeply understand the values and priorities of the kingdom of God? In Matthew 13:52, we have Jesus' answer to that question: "He said to them, 'Therefore every teacher of the law who has been instructed about the kingdom of heaven is like the owner of a house who brings out of his storeroom new treasures as well as old.' "

Ask something like:

▶ **So what happens when you understand and follow the ways of Jesus' family?**
▶ **What happens when you live like a brother or sister of Jesus—as someone shaped by the values and practices of his and your true home?**

After a few responses, if necessary, *add this insight:*

When you adopt the "family system" of the kingdom of God, you can give others what they need whenever they need it. You become like a generous, well-stocked storeroom, full of the "fruits of the spirit"—love, joy, peace, patience, kindness, self-control, and so on. Our purpose is to give "out of our good treasure." But we don't have treasure to give unless we live in the "treasure house"—the kingdom of God.

GOD IS LIKE...(15 MINUTES)

Now that participants have explored some "Kingdom of God" parables, they'll do the same with some "Character of God" parables. This will help them more deeply taste the personality characteristics shared by the Father, Son, and Holy Spirit. Assign each trio one of the parables from the "Character of God" list in their booklets on page 27 (they're also in this leaders guide on page 66). Then instruct trios to read their assigned parable and list as many truths as they can glean about the nature, personality, values, priorities, and passions of the person of God.

- ▶ Parable of the Great Physician—Matthew 9:10-13: Healer and inviter of the outsider.
- ▶ Parable of the Moneylender—Luke 7:40-47: Appreciator of the desperate and indebted.
- ▶ Parable of the Lost Sheep—Luke 15:3-7: Pursuer of lost valuables; partier.
- ▶ Parable of the Lost Coin—Luke 15:8-10: Diligent, won't give up until he finds what he's looking for.
- ▶ Parable of the Prodigal Son—Luke 15:11-32: Forgiving, passionate, just, non-controlling, full of grace and truth, firm, sees the heart, celebrates repentance.

After five minutes or so, ask a spokesperson from each trio to tell about the parable they studied and what truths their trio gleaned about the character of God. Remember to follow The Rules of Engagement.

THE PARABLES CONTINUE (15 MINUTES)

Transition out of the discussion on character of God parables by *saying something like:*

> **Through the parables in the Bible, Jesus reveals his Father's nature and shows what life is like in his kingdom. Jesus continues to tell parables today, right now, in our lives.**
>
> **The best films basically serve as great parables. The best personal stories are great parables. Like radio waves, parables literally surround us. Right now, radio waves flow through this room, but we can't access the message they communicate because we can't tune in**

to them. The same holds true with parables—God is always trying to converse with us and teach us. But are we tuned in?

In just a moment, I want you to take a few minutes to ask God to bring to your mind an event that happened to you in the last week. This might be anything that sticks out to you. Write a short description of the event or happening. Don't think too hard about this. Just write down a few words or sentences about the first thing that comes to your mind. Ready? Go!

After a few minutes, *say something like:*

Now take a few minutes to ask God how this event or happening might be a parable in your life. How is God's voice or message to you locked up in the story?

How does your little parable-story answer one of these two questions:

▶ Who is God?
▶ What is life like in God's kingdom?

I don't want you to "create" the meaning behind the story. Instead, simply ask God to show you the meaning. Wait quietly until you sense the meaning coming to the surface of your mind, and then write the meaning in your personal journey guide.

Remember, we're just playing here. There's nothing on the line. You might not sense any parable connection to your story. Don't try to manufacture one. Just wait with a sense of faith and see what surfaces. Remember, you want God to reveal if your parable story says something about his character or his kingdom.

After a few minutes, ask one or two people to report on what they discovered. If they don't make the connection, you should help find the connection to one of the two big questions parables answer: "What is God like?" and "What is life like in God's kingdom?"

Then say something like:

The more you tune yourself to the parables in your life, the more you'll know who Jesus is. You'll experience more intimacy with Jesus. The parables of Scripture and the parables of your life are God's attempt to have intimate conversation with you.

I'm going to play a song as our closing today. I invite you to enter into the spirit of this song as your own response to God.

Play "Step By Step" by Rich Mullins as a closing response to God.

"GRACE" BY U2

(Song Summary)

This song is about grace—it could be a name or it could be an idea.

Grace "takes the blame" and "covers the shame" and "removes the stain."

Grace is both a girl's name and an act of God that rescued us all.

Grace is beautiful—the most beautiful thing—because grace can take what's ugly and make it beautiful.

Grace knows how to act in every situation—and grace knows how to patiently pursue us.

Grace has nothing to do with the "you get what you deserve" system of the world.

When you're experiencing grace, you can sense God's beauty—because God's grace "finds beauty in everything."

Grace is a working mother—the grace of God is at work in the down-and-dirty of our lives. Her hands are those of a hard worker, not a privileged queen.

Grace points, always, to the pearl of great price, who is Jesus himself. Jesus takes away the "stain" of our sin through grace.

Because we've all been made beautiful by God's grace—he's taken the "ugly" we've offered him (all we have) and made it good.

STRANGE CUSTOMS

All cultures have their "norms," but they can seem bizarre or even disgusting to those not native to the culture. For example…

• In India many use a jug of water and their left palm instead of toilet paper. In Indonesia some use a long fingernail on their left hand for the same purpose—that's why you're never offered a left hand in greeting.

• In Papua New Guinea people squat to use the toilet because it sits level to the ground with two concave footholds on either side.

• In Thailand it's considered rude to cross your legs in the company of others because your toes, the lowest part of your body, are pointing at your guest—that's considered demeaning.

• In Yemen the genders are strictly kept from contact with one another—that's why many marriages are arranged by both the father and mother. Mothers pick brides for their sons, and fathers pick grooms for their daughters.

• If you're a tourist in Japan and you motion with a curved finger to beckon someone to come to you, it's considered as vulgar to the Japanese as a pointed middle finger is in Western culture.

• In Asia some people believe that pearls, either ground into powder or swallowed whole, have medicinal qualities that can heal whatever ails them.

KINGDOM OF GOD PARABLES

THE PARABLE OF WHEAT AND WEEDS

Matthew 13:24-30 (The Message)

He told another story. "God's kingdom is like a farmer who planted good seed in his field. That night, while his hired men were asleep, his enemy sowed thistles all through the wheat and slipped away before dawn. When the first green shoots appeared and the grain began to form, the thistles showed up, too.

"The farmhands came to the farmer and said, 'Master, that was clean seed you planted, wasn't it? Where did these thistles come from?' He answered, 'Some enemy did this.' The farmhands asked, 'Should we weed out the thistles?'

"He said, 'No, if you weed the thistles, you'll pull up the wheat, too. Let them grow together until harvest time. Then I'll instruct the harvesters to pull up the thistles and tie them in bundles for the fire, then gather the wheat and put it in the barn.' "

THE PARABLE OF THE PINE NUT

Matthew 13:31-32 (The Message)

Another story. "God's kingdom is like a pine nut that a farmer plants. It is quite small as seeds go, but in the course of years it grows into a huge pine tree, and eagles build nests in it."

THE PARABLE OF THE YEAST

Matthew 13:33 (The Message)

Another story. "God's kingdom is like yeast that a woman works into the dough for dozens of loaves of barley bread—and waits while the dough rises."

THE PARABLE OF THE TREASURE IN THE FIELD

Matthew 13:44 (The Message)

"God's kingdom is like a treasure hidden in a field for years and then accidentally found by a trespasser. The finder is ecstatic—what a find!—and proceeds to sell everything he owns to raise money and buy that field."

THE PARABLE OF THE PEARL OF GREAT PRICE

Matthew 13:45-46 (The Message)

"Or, God's kingdom is like a jewel merchant on the hunt for excellent pearls. Finding one that is flawless, he immediately sells everything and buys it."

THE PARABLE OF THE BIG FISHNET

Matthew 13:47-50 (The Message)

"Or, God's kingdom is like a fishnet cast into the sea, catching all kinds of fish. When it is full, it is hauled onto the beach. The good fish are picked out and put in a tub; those unfit to eat are thrown away. That's how it will be when the curtain comes down on history. The angels will come and cull the bad fish and throw them in the garbage. There will be a lot of desperate complaining, but it won't do any good."

CHARACTER OF GOD PARABLES

PARABLE OF THE GREAT PHYSICIAN
Matthew 9:10-13 (The Message)

Later when Jesus was eating supper at Matthew's house with his close followers, a lot of disreputable characters came and joined them. When the Pharisees saw him keeping this kind of company, they had a fit, and lit into Jesus' followers. "What kind of example is this from your Teacher, acting cozy with crooks and riffraff?" Jesus, overhearing, shot back, "Who needs a doctor: the healthy or the sick? Go figure out what this Scripture means: 'I'm after mercy, not religion.' I'm here to invite outsiders, not coddle insiders."

PARABLE OF THE MONEYLENDER
Luke 7:40-47 (The Message)

Jesus said to him, "Simon, I have something to tell you." "Oh? Tell me." "Two men were in debt to a banker. One owed five hundred silver pieces, the other fifty. Neither of them could pay up, and so the banker canceled both debts. Which of the two would be more grateful?" Simon answered, "I suppose the one who was forgiven the most." "That's right," said Jesus. Then turning to the woman, but speaking to Simon, he said, "Do you see this woman? I came to your home; you provided no water for my feet, but she rained tears on my feet and dried them with her hair. You gave me no greeting, but from the time I arrived she hasn't quit kissing my feet. You provided nothing for freshening up, but she has soothed my feet with perfume. Impressive, isn't it? She was forgiven many, many sins, and so she is very, very grateful. If the forgiveness is minimal, the gratitude is minimal."

THE PARABLE OF THE LOST SHEEP

Luke 15:3-7 (The Message)

By this time a lot of men and women of doubtful reputation were hanging around Jesus, listening intently. The Pharisees and religion scholars were not pleased, not at all pleased. They growled, "He takes in sinners and eats meals with them, treating them like old friends." Their grumbling triggered this story.

"Suppose one of you had a hundred sheep and lost one. Wouldn't you leave the ninety-nine in the wilderness and go after the lost one until you found it? When found, you can be sure you would put it across your shoulders, rejoicing, and when you got home call in your friends and neighbors, saying, 'Celebrate with me! I've found my lost sheep!' Count on it—there's more joy in heaven over one sinner's rescued life than over ninety-nine good people in no need of rescue."

THE PARABLE OF THE LOST COIN

Luke 15:8-10 (The Message)

"Or imagine a woman who has ten coins and loses one. Won't she light a lamp and scour the house, looking in every nook and cranny until she finds it? And when she finds it you can be sure she'll call her friends and neighbors: 'Celebrate with me! I found my lost coin!' Count on it—that's the kind of party God's angels throw every time one lost soul turns to God."

THE PARABLE OF THE PRODIGAL SON

Luke 15:11-32 (The Message)

Then he said, "There was once a man who had two sons. The younger said to his father, 'Father, I want right now what's coming to me.' So the father divided the property between them. It wasn't long before the younger son packed his bags and left for a distant country. There, undisciplined and dissipated, he wasted everything he had. After he had gone through all his money, there was a bad famine all through that country and he began to hurt. He signed on with a citizen there who assigned him to his fields to slop the pigs. He was so hungry he would have eaten the corncobs in the pig slop, but no one would give him any. That brought him to his senses. He said, 'All those farmhands working for my father sit down to three meals a day, and here I am starving to death. I'm going back to my father. I'll say to him, Father, I've sinned against God, I've sinned before you; I don't deserve to be called your son. Take me on as a hired hand.' He got right up and went home to his father. When he was still a long way off, his father saw him. His heart pounding, he ran out, embraced him, and kissed him. The son started his speech: 'Father, I've sinned against God, I've sinned before you; I don't deserve to be called your son ever again.' But the father wasn't listening. He was calling to the servants, 'Quick. Bring a clean set of clothes and dress him. Put the family ring on his finger and sandals on his feet. Then get a grain-fed heifer and roast it. We're going to feast! We're going to have a wonderful time! My son is here—given up for dead and now alive! Given up for lost and now found!' And they began to have a wonderful time. All this time his older son was out in the field. When the day's work was done he came in. As he approached the house, he heard the music and dancing. Calling over one of the houseboys, he asked what was going on. He told him, 'Your brother came home. Your father has ordered a feast—barbecued beef!—because he has him home safe and sound.' The older brother stalked off in an angry sulk and refused to join in. His father came out and tried to talk to him, but he wouldn't listen. The son said, 'Look how many years I've stayed here serving you, never giving you one moment of grief, but have you ever thrown a party for me and my friends? Then this son of yours who has thrown away your money on whores shows up and you go all out with a feast!' His father said, 'Son, you don't understand. You're with me all the time, and everything that is mine is yours—but this is a wonderful time, and we had to celebrate. This brother of yours was dead, and he's alive! He was lost, and he's found!' "

IN PURSUIT OF JESUS

WEEK 4: JESUS AND THE DESPERATE PEOPLE

PRIOR TO THIS SESSION

- ▷ Set up a boombox or stereo system to play music.
- ▷ Set up a white board or big pad of paper, along with markers.
- ▷ Set up a VCR or DVD player connected to a TV or a projector to show the film clip.
- ▷ Cue up track 11, "The Silence of God," on Andrew Peterson's *Love and Thunder* CD for your opening worship. You'll also play track 6, "Just As I Am," for your closing worship.
- ▷ Provide a small paper cup with a small amount of salt in it for each participant.
- ▷ Provide a small paper cup of water for each participant.
- ▷ Cue up the bar scene with George Bailey from the film *It's a Wonderful Life* (1:35:23–1:37:30 on the DVD).

WELCOME AND INTRODUCTION (25 MINUTES)

When people arrive welcome them. Then give each person a small cup with some salt in it. Ask participants to put a pinch of salt on their tongues then close their eyes and listen to the song.

Now play "The Silence of God" by Andrew Peterson.

As the song ends, tell people to keep their eyes closed while you read aloud (*very slowly, with meaning*) John 7:37:

"Now on the last day, the great day of the feast, Jesus stood and cried out, saying, 'If anyone is thirsty, let him come to Me and drink' " (NAS).

Then pause in silence for about 10 seconds.

Then ask these questions for people to ponder quietly, pausing for 10 to 15 seconds between each question:

- ▶ **Are we aware of how thirsty our souls are?**
- ▶ **What is your soul thirsty for?**
- ▶ **What do you typically do to quench that thirst?**
- ▶ **What kind of water does Jesus offer us?**

Instruct participants to open their eyes. Tell them you know they're probably thirsty right now, but to wait to get a drink. *Then say something like:*

If you think about many of the interactions Jesus had, the stories he told, and the life he lived, desperation is a part of all of them. It's really a central aspect of most of his relationships. Desperation is also the theme of his most famous parable, the parable of the prodigal son.

Desperation is like a basic thirst. And desperation often crawls into the shadows of our lives, too.

Now briefly share (taking no more than five minutes) your own experience or example of desperation in life (for example, a relational hardship, a health concern, or any other significant challenge in your life). The closer to the present the better, because it's far easier and safer to share a story from 10 years ago. Talk about your experience with desperation: What did you do to deal with it? What did you learn from it? What are your feelings about it today? Finally, talk about how during this time of desperation, you focused on Jesus (or didn't).

End your story by reading aloud Psalm 42:1-2a:

"As the deer pants for the water brooks, So my soul pants for You, O God. My soul thirsts for God, for the living God" (NAS).

Then say something like:

Desperation is also a central element in nearly every good film, because we're drawn to people facing desperation. We're fascinated by how people respond to desperation. We're eager to learn from their responses.

Let's watch one of my favorite desperation scenes from a movie.

SHOW FILM CLIP

Show Jimmy Stewart in the bar scene from *It's a Wonderful Life* (cue up the DVD to 1:35:23, then play the scene to 1:37:30).

After the clip, instruct people to pair up (remember to separate spouses). Then have pairs discuss these questions:

- ▶ Can you think of a time in your life you felt something like what George Bailey felt in this scene?
- ▶ Was the "fruit" or result of that desperation good or bad in your life? Explain.

After seven minutes or so, get the group's attention again.

THE ROOTS AND ROLE OF DESPERATION (10 MINUTES)

Say something like:

We almost always know the short-term causes of why we feel desperate—a lost job, financial trouble, or a child struggling with addiction. But we don't always know the root of our desperation at a deeper level.

If we look at our history as human beings—all the way back to Adam and Eve—we find all the clues we need. Adam and Eve gave in to the temptation of sin because, essentially, they wanted to be equal to God.

Read aloud Genesis 3:1-5. Tell participants they can read along in their participant booklets:

"Now the serpent was more crafty than any of the wild animals the Lord God had made. He said to the woman, 'Did God really say, "You must not eat from any tree in the garden"?' The woman said to the serpent, 'We may eat fruit from the trees in the garden, but God did say, "You must not eat fruit from the tree that is in the middle of the garden, and you must not touch it, or you will die." ' 'You will not surely die,' the serpent said to the woman. 'For God knows that when you eat of it your eyes will be opened, and you will be like God, knowing good and evil.' "

Then say something like:

We all know what happens next! Eve ate the fruit, and then gave it to Adam to eat. Because of what Satan told her—or dangled in front of her—she's drawn to the forbidden fruit. What draws her?

Satan promises she can become like God—self-sufficient and in charge of her own destiny. Adam quickly follows her lead. Together, they put their faith in the false hope that they can be gods. But in the kingdom of God, if you believe you're a god, you're outside of relationship with the one true God.

 We're literally sick with the myth of our own self-sufficiency. Desperation serves as a medicine that can help make us well. This feeling reminds us that we're not God—we never have been, we're not right now, and we never will be. It tells us we're not in control.

Story: Heather, who cut my hair. Cocaine addict — landed in jail. Every woman tries. project day.

If you want, tell a recent news story about someone who lived self-sufficiently, by his or her own rules. When that person became desperate, he or she finally turned to God.

Or tell a classic story instead. The story of John Newton's conversion is a good example; Newton wrote the hymn "Amazing Grace." You can find a succinct version of this story at www.wikipedia.org—just search for "John Newton."

People who are not desperate, or those who won't move beyond their false belief of their own god-ness because of desperation, live in bondage to a lie. They say they don't need God. But deep down they doubt their own claims. Desperation becomes the open door, the open window, to the truth, to true freedom: I am not God, I've never been God, I don't want to be God. I am simply a branch that will die apart from the vine, who is Jesus (see John 15:5).

During Jesus' ministry on earth, the people who seemed to "get" this also got to hang out with Jesus. Jesus preferred hanging out with desperate people. They were his closest friends—his disciples. Jesus was drawn to their desperate hearts like a magnet.

THE DESPERADOES AND THE PHARISEES (40 MINUTES)

Ask participants to take a deeper dive into the stories of desperate people in Scripture. Have them take five minutes or so to read through the stories of "The Desperadoes" in their booklets on pages 37-39. Ask them to look at the role desperation might have played in the relationships these people had with Jesus. If participants notice something, they can either write a note in their booklet or simply circle it in the stories.

The Desperadoes include:

- ▶ The disciples who dropped everything to follow Jesus
- ▶ The woman who touched the hem of Jesus' garment
- ▶ The prostitute at the party of Pharisees
- ▶ Zacchaeus the tax collector
- ▶ The Canaanite woman.

After five minutes, *say something like:*

Something sets these people apart from the others surrounding Jesus. Something motivated them to do what they did. Clearly, Jesus was drawn to these people. He had a completely different reaction to them than he had to the Pharisees. With these "teachers of the law," Jesus was often frustrated, angry, and even harsh because of their hypocritical, judgmental, and rule-keeping attitudes.

Let's compare and contrast what we know of both kinds of people.

On your white board or pad, make two columns separated by a vertical line. Title one column "Desperadoes" and the other "Pharisees."

Then ask these questions:

- ▶ **What was different about the people we're calling the Desperadoes, compared to what we know about the Pharisees?**
- ▶ **How were these individuals different in what they said and did?**
- ▶ **What motivated them that seems different from the Pharisees?**
- ▶ **What drew Jesus to the Desperadoes?**

List what people say for either column. When you get an answer for one column, ask for a comparison to the people in the other column. For example, if someone says the hearts of the Desperadoes were "tender and soft," ask that person or others in the group to compare that description to what they know about the Pharisees' hearts.

THE RULES OF ENGAGEMENT

Whenever you gather input from the whole group—either from a question you ask or as they report back on discussions they have—use these tips to remember how to prime the discussion, ask follow-up questions, and engage the responses you get back:

1. Embrace every answer. Write a condensed version of each one on your white board or pad.
2. If an answer seems vague, confusing, wrong, or sounds like the Sunday school "right" answer, follow up with one of these go-deeper comments or questions:
   ▶ "Please say more about what you mean."
   ▶ "I've never thought of that before—could you explain more?"
   ▶ "That seems to contradict what we commonly believe—could you be more specific?"
   ▶ "That's the answer we expect. How would you explain that to someone who doesn't know the 'expected' answer?"
3. If an answer is surprising or insightful, ask the person to say a little more (unless the answer was detailed in the first place). You can ask others in the group to expand on that answer, too.
4. When someone specifically connects with where the study is headed, highlight that answer as important to pay attention to.
5. Aim for developing an atmosphere that resembles a good conversation, where you and other group members interact all the time with what someone says.

After you collect and pursue many answers, *ask something like:*

▶ **Why did Jesus gravitate to and honor the Desperadoes? What about Jesus draws him to these people?**

Write their answers on your white board or pad. Remember to use The Rules of Engagement.

After you list a few responses, *offer this insight if no one else does:*

> We love to hang out with people who see us well: people who are truthful and loving mirrors of who we are; people who enjoy us for who we really are. That's what makes intimacy possible.
>
> And desperate people see Jesus well. They know they're not God. They know that Jesus *is* God. They sense that he's the source of their life and that they need him. They base their relationship with him on the truth. This allows them to have an intimate relationship with him.

Ask the following rhetorical questions *(no need for participants to answer out loud):*

> ▶ Why do we hate the feeling of desperation?
> ▶ If desperation is an open door to our heart that Jesus can walk through, how do we invite him in?

Say something like:

> The great Oswald Chambers, author of *My Utmost for His Highest,* took a stab at answering these questions. Right now, close your eyes and listen as I read what Chambers titled "Receiving Yourself in the Fires of Sorrow."

Read aloud "Receiving Yourself in the Fires of Sorrow" by Oswald Chambers (found on page 80).

Then ask something like:

> ▶ Chambers said that "suffering either gives me to myself or it destroys me." Why do you think this is true? What does it mean to "receive ourselves" in our suffering?

CLOSING WORSHIP

After a few responses, give each person a small cup of water. Direct participants to the song summary of Andrew Peterson's song "Just As I Am" on page 42 in their booklets (or get the actual lyrics by going to our Web site at www.pursuitofjesus.com and clicking on the link for them). Ask them to get comfortable and either close their eyes or read the summary or lyrics as they listen to the song. Invite them to sip the water as they listen.

After the song, close in prayer. If you like, you can repeat a variation of the opening meditation. Read each question, pausing to allow participants time to consider each one. They can respond to Jesus directly and silently:

> ▶ **How is Jesus quenching your thirst right now?**
> ▶ **Is anything keeping you from fully giving in to your thirst for Jesus right now? If so, what?**
> ▶ **What do you appreciate about the water Jesus offers you?**

THE DESPERADOES

> ▶ **The Disciples** (Matthew 4:18-22): "As Jesus was walking beside the Sea of Galilee, he saw two brothers, Simon called Peter and his brother Andrew. They were casting a net into the lake, for they were fishermen. 'Come, follow me,' Jesus said, 'and I will make you fishers of men.' At once they left their nets and followed him. Going on from there, he saw two other brothers, James son of Zebedee and his brother John. They were in a boat with their father Zebedee, preparing their nets. Jesus called them, and immediately they left the boat and their father and followed him."
>
> ▶ **The Woman With an Issue of Blood** (Matthew 9:18-22)—"While he was saying this, a ruler came and knelt before him and said, 'My daughter has just died. But come and put your hand on her, and she will live.' Jesus got up and went with him, and so did his disciples. Just then a woman who had been sub-ject to bleeding for twelve years came up behind him and touched the edge of his cloak. She said to herself, 'If I only touch his cloak, I will be healed.' Jesus

turned and saw her. 'Take heart, daughter,' he said, 'your faith has healed you.' And the woman was healed from that moment."

▶ **The Sinful Woman at the Pharisee's Party** (Luke 7:36-50)—"Now one of the Pharisees invited Jesus to have dinner with him, so he went to the Pharisee's house and reclined at the table. When a woman who had lived a sinful life in that town learned that Jesus was eating at the Pharisee's house, she brought an alabaster jar of perfume, and as she stood behind him at his feet weeping, she began to wet his feet with her tears. Then she wiped them with her hair, kissed them and poured perfume on them. When the Pharisee who had invited him saw this, he said to himself, 'If this man were a prophet, he would know who is touching him and what kind of woman she is—that she is a sinner.' Jesus answered him, 'Simon, I have something to tell you.' 'Tell me, teacher,' he said. 'Two men owed money to a certain moneylender. One owed him five hundred denarii, and the other fifty. Neither of them had the money to pay him back, so he canceled the debts of both. Now which of them will love him more?' Simon replied, 'I suppose the one who had the bigger debt canceled.' 'You have judged correctly,' Jesus said. Then he turned toward the woman and said to Simon, 'Do you see this woman? I came into your house. You did not give me any water for my feet, but she wet my feet with her tears and wiped them with her hair. You did not give me a kiss, but this woman, from the time I entered, has not stopped kissing my feet. You did not put oil on my head, but she has poured perfume on my feet. Therefore, I tell you, her many sins have been forgiven—for she loved much. But he who has been forgiven little loves little.' Then Jesus said to her, 'Your sins are forgiven.' The other guests began to say among themselves, 'Who is this who even forgives sins?' Jesus said to the woman, 'Your faith has saved you; go in peace.' "

▶ **Zacchaeus the Tax Collector** (Luke 19:1-10)—"Jesus entered Jericho and was passing through. A man was there by the name of Zacchaeus; he was a chief tax collector and was wealthy. He wanted to see who Jesus was, but being a short man he could not, because of the crowd. So he ran ahead and climbed a sycamore-fig tree to see him, since Jesus was coming that way. When Jesus reached the spot, he looked up and said to him, 'Zacchaeus, come down immediately. I must stay at your house today.' So he came down at once and welcomed him gladly. All the people saw this and began to mutter, 'He has gone to be the guest of a "sinner." ' But Zacchaeus stood up and said to the Lord, 'Look, Lord! Here and now I give half of my possessions to the poor, and if I have cheated anybody out of anything, I will pay back four times the amount.' Jesus said to him, 'Today salvation has come to this house, because this man, too, is a son of Abraham. For the Son of Man came to seek and to save what was lost.' "

▷ **The Canaanite Woman** (Matthew 15:21-28)—"Leaving that place, Jesus withdrew to the region of Tyre and Sidon. A Canaanite woman from that vicinity came to him, crying out, 'Lord, Son of David, have mercy on me! My daughter is suffering terribly from demon-possession.' Jesus did not answer a word. So his disciples came to him and urged him, 'Send her away, for she keeps crying out after us.' He answered, 'I was sent only to the lost sheep of Israel.' The woman came and knelt before him. 'Lord, help me!' she said. He replied, 'It is not right to take the children's bread and toss it to their dogs.' 'Yes, Lord,' she said, 'but even the dogs eat the crumbs that fall from their masters' table.' Then Jesus answered, 'Woman, you have great faith! Your request is granted.' And her daughter was healed from that very hour."

RECEIVING YOURSELF IN THE FIRES OF SORROW[1]

Oswald Chambers

June 25

"What shall I say? 'Father, save Me from this hour'? But for this purpose I came to this hour. 'Father, glorify Your name'" (John 12:27-28).

As a saint of God, my attitude toward sorrow and difficulty should not be to ask that they be prevented, but to ask that God protect me so that I may remain what He created me to be, in spite of all my fires of sorrow. Our Lord received Himself, accepting His position and realizing His purpose, in the midst of the fire of sorrow. He was saved not from the hour, but out of the hour.

We say that there ought to be no sorrow, but there is sorrow, and we have to accept and receive ourselves in its fires. If we try to evade sorrow, refusing to deal with it, we are foolish. Sorrow is one of the biggest facts in life, and there is no use in saying it should not be. Sin, sorrow, and suffering are, and it is not for us to say that God has made a mistake in allowing them.

Sorrow removes a great deal of a person's shallowness, but it does not always make that person better. Suffering either gives me to myself or it destroys me. You cannot find or receive yourself through success, because you lose your head over pride. And you cannot receive yourself through the monotony of your daily life, because you give in to complaining. The only way to find yourself is in the fires of sorrow. Why it should be this way is immaterial. The fact is that it is true in the Scriptures and in human experience. You can always recognize who has been through the fires of sorrow and received himself, and you know that you can go to him in your moment of trouble and find that he has plenty of time for you. But if a person has not been through the fires of sorrow, he is apt to be contemptuous, having no respect or time for you, only turning you away.

If you will receive yourself in the fires of sorrow, God will make you nourishment for other people.

"THE SILENCE OF GOD" BY ANDREW PETERSON

(Song Summary)

When you're desperately hurting and craving God's comfort and strength, it can literally break you to hear only silence in response to your cries.

It can seem impossible to get your mind off of the things that are crushing your spirit.

Even though Jesus has told us his "yoke is easy" and his "burden is light," it often seems as though our burdens are way too heavy for us—especially when God seems absent or distant to us.

It's even harder to see other Christians apparently enjoying all the good things life has to offer—health and wealth and happiness—and have to listen to them piously tell you that Jesus has taken away all their troubles.

But you know the truth—everyone must wrestle with sorrow and trouble, and even those who follow Christ can lose their way.

It's easy to forget that Jesus experienced great troubles—think of his desperation in the Garden of Gethsemane, when he knew the horror he was about to face and yet not one of his best friends could stay awake to be with him. He's alone there, in the tyranny of the silence.

So Jesus understands—deeply—the silence and sorrow we sometimes bear alone.

God does not abandon us in that silence—soon our aching questions fade in importance, replaced by his intimate presence. Our sorrows don't have to break us—they can lead us into the very presence of God.

"JUST AS I AM" BY ANDREW PETERSON

(Song Summary)

Jesus is a heartbreaker—not, of course, in the romantic sense. But when we love him, he breaks our hearts. And he takes the broken bits and makes something beautiful grow out of them.

It's incredible that Jesus is able to take our heartbreaks and transform them into something beautiful.

Jesus has proved, over and over and over, that he knows us intimately and loves us deeply.

But we have a deep anxiety that all that is beautiful in our lives—all of the beauty Jesus is growing—can be taken away by our own terrible choices. We fear that there are limits to God's love for us, that it's ultimately a conditional love and he expects us to perform well to get it.

But then we remember the great sacrifices of Jesus, and we remember that there are no lengths he will not go to in his pursuit of us. We are loved, truly.

The "seeds" of love Jesus has planted in our lives do bear "fruit," and Jesus longs to use that fruit for the good of others in our lives. But he's not in love with our fruit—he's in love with us. He loves us, truly.

ENDNOTE 1: Taken from *My Utmost for His Highest* by Oswald Chambers, edited by James Reimann, © 1992 by Oswald Chambers Publications Assn., Ltd., and used by permission of Discovery House Publishers, Grand Rapids MI 49501. All rights reserved.

WEEK 5: JESUS AND HIS FAMILY

PRIOR TO THIS SESSION

- ▶ Set up a boombox or stereo system, ready to play music.
- ▶ Set up a white board or big pad of paper, along with markers.
- ▶ Set up a VCR or DVD player connected to a TV or a projector to show the film clip.
- ▶ Cue up track 7, "Mighty Is the Power of the Cross," on Chris Tomlin's *Arriving* CD for your closing worship.
- ▶ Cue up the clip from the 2003 film *Cheaper By the Dozen* (47:10 to 49:00 on the DVD). In this scene, Tom Baker, football coach and father of 12 kids, tries to prepare dinner and take care of all the household needs while his wife is away. Of course, chaos ensues.
- ▶ Provide a cutting from a small tree, bush, or shrub for each participant. A cutting is just a small branch, which you can find by pruning your own foliage at home. Or go to a plant nursery and ask for cuttings. If these options won't work for you, ask a flower shop for greenery (even leftover cuttings). Cut the stems so they have a fresh cut. Whichever option you choose, bring the cuttings in a paper bag, and hide them so participants don't see them in advance.

WELCOME AND INTRODUCTION (15 MINUTES)

After you welcome people to the study, tell them you're going to start with a film clip. You don't really need to set up this clip more than that.

SHOW FILM CLIP

Show a scene from *Cheaper By the Dozen*. Cue the DVD to 47:10, when Tom is cooking dinner, and stop it at 49:00, when Tom puts the bandage on his daughter's forehead.

Say something like:

> Does this remind you of your family at all? I wonder if it would remind Jesus of his family. Do you think Jesus grew up in a "normal" family? Think back to what we talked about in week 3, "Jesus and His Parables." We learned that God wants to relate with us so much that he made the whole world full of parables—stories that reveal his heart and the values of his kingdom.
>
> Every created thing can reveal truths about God and his kingdom. This is profoundly true when we consider families. What if God places us into families as parables, to help us understand some of what living in the family of God is like?
>
> Jesus himself was born into a family. God intended that he grow up in a home with parents. In fact, family relationships dominate Jesus' life.
>
> Let's spend some time thinking about your own relationship to family throughout your life. On page 43 of your booklet, you'll find a list of film and TV families. Each one represents a type of family. Scan the list right now and pick the one that best represents the family you grew up in. If you don't find one that kind of fits, think of a family from a TV show or film that does remind you of your family. Take a moment to choose the one that best fits your family of origin—the family you grew up in as a child.

Give participants just one minute to make a choice, and then *say something like:*

> Now get together with a partner—someone you haven't paired up with so far in this series. Share the family you chose, and tell why that TV or film family has similarities to your own. Go!

THERE'S NO PLACE LIKE HOME

Which family comes closest to describing your family? Choose one (or choose your own TV/film family) that comes closest to the kind of family you grew up in.

- *The Bradys (The Brady Bunch)*—Middle-class blended family with some sibling friction, but an underlying sense of togetherness. Strong personalities and adventurous spirits. Strong, engaged father and mother who are generally easy-going—never too intense.

- *The Simpsons (The Simpsons)*—Typically dysfunctional family, but not in a terribly damaging way. The problems of the parents and the kids don't obscure their ultimate underlying love and commitment to each other. One parent is a loose cannon and the other is the steadying influence in the family. Some kids are high achievers, others are not. Sometimes it seems like the family is barely holding together, yet they seem to work out their problems.

- *The Sopranos (The Sopranos)*—A highly dysfunctional family with damaging and even dangerous relationships. The family holds together, but not because of warm, intimate love for each other. Rather, fear and survival characterize the home environment. Betrayal, lying, and pragmatic brutality overshadow family closeness, though everyone seems to want it.

- *The Huxtables (The Cosby Show)*—Laughter-filled middle-class home with a strong, professional father and a nurturing, professional mother. Strong values, high expectations, and relational strength saturate the home environment. Bad decisions result in consequences that the parents won't circumvent. This home represents a "teachable moment" kind of climate. Of course, sometimes things seem almost too perfect.

- *The Waltons (The Waltons)*—A poor, hardworking, but close-knit family. Even extended family members live together. A strong work ethic and family values characterize the family, but faith in Christ seems to be more of a cultural expectation than a personal commitment. Large age span among the children, so older kids often participate in the rearing of the younger ones.

▶ *The von Trapps (Sound of Music)*—A family hurting from loss and sorrow, trying to cope and find their way through the darkness. The normal family system is rigid and authoritarian as a result of the wounding. One person in the family offers hope, light, and love as an alternate path.

▶ *The Addams (The Addams Family)*—A family full of strange and over-the-top characters who somehow all fit together. A lot of bizarre experiences characterize the growing-up years. The family "norms" seem outlandish to people outside the family, but family members have a general respect and acceptance of one another. This family has fun, but not in traditional ways.

▶ *The Camdens (7th Heaven)*—A strong religious household where the church and faith occupy a central place in the family's life. While the family encounters many challenges, sorrows, and joys in life, they hold together because of the parents' strength of conviction. This largely functional home still has moments of dysfunction. Parents not only tolerate doubts, struggles, and even contrary views, they explore and accept those in the family context.

JESUS AND HIS FAMILIES (35 MINUTES)

After pairs take five minutes to talk about how the family they chose is similar to their own, *say something like:*

> **Let's remind ourselves of the point of our 10-week pursuit—to answer Jesus' central question to us: "Who do you say I am?" You can learn a lot about people when you get to know their family. Right now, you know a lot more about your partner than you did a few minutes ago because you heard some things about his or her family.**
>
> **When you think about it, Jesus really has *three* families. First, he has a heavenly family, including the Father and the Holy Spirit. We talked about this Trinity in our parables study. Jesus also has a human family of origin—Mary and Joseph and some brothers. And he has a**

third family that he calls his true family. In this study, we'll focus on Jesus' earthly family and his true family.

The church elevates the idea of family—calling for a certain standard of family and a certain attention on family as crucial to living the Christian life. Jesus valued family, too, but in a different way than we typically do in the church. In fact, one of the more radical things he ever did was to redefine family.

In this session, you'll take participants to a deeper level into the connections Jesus had to family—both his human family and his "true family."

First, instruct participants to get back with their partners from the opening discussion about families, then assign each pair one of the Family Matters stories to read on page 48 in their booklets (if you have more pairs than stories, simply assign some stories to more than one pair; if you have fewer pairs than stories, simply give pairs more than one story to read). Be sure each pair has at least one Bible. Encourage them to first read the story from their booklets, and then (if they want) reference the context of the story from the Bible later during their discussion.

After pairs read their assigned stories, have them *discuss this question:*

In your story, what can you learn about Jesus' relationship to family? In other words, what can you learn about the nature of his family relationships—his attitude toward family and his definition of family—from your story?

Ask participants to write their insights in their booklets. Remind them that if their story seems too thin or too easy, they should slow down, pay attention, fuel their curiosity, and look for unexplored insights and questions. For example, if a pair reads the story of Jesus' genealogy, they might not think they can learn anything specific about his family from a list. However, if they slow down and pay close attention to the list, they might find some surprises in Jesus' family tree. So they can dig deeper and ask what it means that Jesus has some reprobate people feeding into his family of origin. If a pair feels stuck, urge them to stop and simply ask God to show them the hidden treasure in their story.

THE RULES OF ENGAGEMENT

Whenever you gather input from the whole group—either from a question you ask or as they report back on discussions they have—use these tips to remember how to prime the discussion, ask follow-up questions, and engage the responses you get back:

1. Embrace every answer. Write a condensed version of each one on your white board or pad.
2. If an answer seems vague, confusing, wrong, or sounds like the Sunday school "right" answer, follow up with one of these go-deeper comments or questions:
   - ▶ "Please say more about what you mean."
   - ▶ "I've never thought of that before—could you explain more?"
   - ▶ "That seems to contradict what we commonly believe—could you be more specific?"
   - ▶ "That's the answer we expect. How would you explain that to someone who doesn't know the 'expected' answer?"
3. If an answer is surprising or insightful, ask the person to say a little more (unless the answer was detailed in the first place). You can ask others in the group to expand on that answer, too.
4. When someone specifically connects with where the study is headed, highlight that answer as important to pay attention to.
5. Aim for developing an atmosphere that resembles a good conversation, where you and other group members interact all the time with what someone says.

While pairs discuss their stories, write the following headings on your white board or pad. Leave space under each heading to write a few responses from participants:

- ▶ Jesus' Genealogy
- ▶ Jesus Stays Behind at the Temple
- ▶ Jesus Turns Water into Wine
- ▶ Jesus and Family Obligations

- ▶ Jesus Comes With a Sword
- ▶ True Mother and Brothers
- ▶ Jesus Creates a New Family

After six minutes or so, ask pairs to report on what they learned from the stories they explored. Go through the stories in order, from the first to last story as listed in "Family Matters." Condense what pairs say about their stories, and write their comments on the white board or pad. Then move to the next pair. Ask questions for clarification if you need to, and occasionally ask the rest of the class to respond to what other pairs found. For example, *ask something like:*

> ▶ **What's new or surprising or uncomfortable or even confusing about what I've written about this Family Matters story?**

Remember that you need to gather insights on seven stories, so don't camp too long on any one of them. However, if one story generates a lot of good discussion about Jesus' relationship to family, don't be afraid to fuel that conversation. You can always make up the time by asking one or two pairs to simply and briefly tell you the "takeaway" from their assigned story, without pursuing it more deeply.

At the end of your journey through the Family Matters stories, *ask something like:*

> ▶ **What can we say, broadly, about Jesus' relationship to family? How would you sum up what we've discovered?**

Remember to follow The Rules of Engagement. After you gather some input, *say something like:*

> **Right around the time of the passage in "The Cost of Following Jesus Includes Family Obligations," Jesus' relationship to family shifts. At this point, he begins to redefine family. Based on our conversations, how would we sum up the way he describes or defines "family"?**

Write a summation statement on your white board or pad based on the input you get from participants.

GRAFTED INTO JESUS' FAMILY (10 MINUTES)

Now the group will explore both what becoming an intimate part of Jesus' "true family" looks like and how it actually happens.

Read aloud John 15:5-8:

> "I am the vine; you are the branches. If a man remains in me and I in him, he will bear much fruit; apart from me you can do nothing. If anyone does not remain in me, he is like a branch that is thrown away and withers; such branches are picked up, thrown into the fire and burned. If you remain in me and my words remain in you, ask whatever you wish, and it will be given you. This is to my Father's glory, that you bear much fruit, showing yourselves to be my disciples."

Explain that Jesus is describing what it's like to be "grafted" into his family. To help the group understand better what this means, read aloud Paul's teaching on "grafting" in Romans 11:17-20, 24:

> "If some of the branches have been broken off, and you, though a wild olive shoot, have been grafted in among the others and now share in the nourishing sap from the olive root, do not boast over those branches. If you do, consider this: You do not support the root, but the root supports you. You will say then, 'Branches were broken off so that I could be grafted in.' Granted. But they were broken off because of unbelief, and you stand by faith. Do not be arrogant, but be afraid. After all, if you were cut out of an olive tree that is wild by nature, and contrary to nature were grafted into a cultivated olive tree, how much more readily will these, the natural branches, be grafted into their own olive tree!"

Now explain how the process of grafting works. *Say something like:*

If you're not an avid gardener, you may have no idea how the process of grafting works. So let me give you an overview. This is how the professionals who work for nurseries describe the process and requirements for grafting:

- First you need a hardy "root stock." This plant is vigorous and full of life energy.

- When you graft, you typically choose a weaker or less hardy plant to graft into the stronger and acclimated root.

- Professionals typically use grafting only when they want to make a hybrid plant: "a new creature." For example, they might create a unique plant that can live and thrive in a particular climate with stronger roots than the original plant's natural ones.

- Grafting is an art. It's not easy to make a graft work. You need to know what you're doing and exercise a lot of patience. If you approach the process quickly or haphazardly, the graft won't take.

- When you graft, you cut a branch from the weaker plant or tree. Then you join that open cut to an open cut on the stronger or root tree. This is an intimate process. It reminds us of what Jesus said: "I am the bridegroom, you are my bride." "I am the vine, you are [my grafted] branches."

- Finally, over time, the life of the grafted branch becomes part of the life of the strong plant or tree. Often, the weaker graft actually falls away after a successful graft. Its life is transferred to the root—hidden in it and part of a new species.

A MEDITATION ON GRAFTING (10 MINUTES)

Play some unobtrusive instrumental music during this meditation and journaling activity. Give each person a small cutting from a shrub or tree. Let participants know that you'll be leading them through a quiet meditation on grafting. You'll ask them to quietly consider some questions while they explore their cut branch. In other words, you *don't* want them to answer out loud.

Remind participants to "play with" this activity and simply do what you ask them to do. Ask them to suspend their right to analyze and criticize and stay distant. Instead, encourage them to "play" by plunging in.

Read aloud or translate into your own words the following meditations, punctuated by significant pauses so people can drink in what you're saying or asking. Speak calmly but loud enough so everyone can hear. *Say something like:*

- ▶ **I'd like you to close your eyes. You're welcome to open them when you want to look more closely at your cutting or write something in your notes—but close them again after that.**
- ▶ **Carefully, slowly feel the surface of the branch and the leaves.**
- ▶ **Now carefully, slowly feel the open cut on your branch. Let yourself linger over the touch, almost as if you were taking its pulse.**
- ▶ **What do you feel? Does it feel tender, vulnerable, exposed, or raw? What other words would you use to describe the cut?**
- ▶ **Now think about this: Sin tore us away from our true Father and grafted us into a family of rebellion. This family is infected with sin. That's why Jesus told those who insisted they didn't need the freedom he was offering them that they belonged to "your father, the devil" (John 8:44).**
- ▶ **Grab a stem on your branch or stalk and tear it from the main branch, and listen to this startling truth: Jesus told us he didn't come to bring peace but a sword. This sword would cut us away from our rebellious family, even though it's the only family we've ever known. Touch the cut on your branch again—imagine what the jolt must have been like when it was cut.**
- ▶ **Remember, Jesus said we are the branches and he is the vine. Imagine that you're just like the cut branch you're holding. You have an open wound. Put the cut end close to your nose and take in the**

smell. If you could, would you try to cover the cut with a scab to protect the wound?

▶ Again, imagining that you're like the branch with an open wound. In order to be grafted into Jesus' strong tree, you'll have to leave your wound open and uncovered. What would it take to leave the wound open so it could be grafted in to a stronger root?

▶ Your open wound makes grafting possible. Don't be afraid of it. It's a gift and an invitation. *(Repeat this point for emphasis.)* **Are you actually searching for the strong vine? Do you long to be grafted to the stronger root…or do you still pine for your old tree?**

▶ The bond of being grafted in to the stronger root is intimate, but it's not instantaneous. It takes a long time to graft. Feel the leaves on your branch. You can sense they're wilting, slowly dying, can't you? That's what happens when a branch is cut…but the life from the root—from Jesus—will transform you. You'll feel new life flowing in you, to make you into a new species. You'll feel it, but it's a slow process to full union with Jesus.

▶ Do you sense evidence of Jesus' new life flowing into you? Are you stronger now that you're part of Jesus' family—now that you're grafted to his root—than you were before? Ask God for the evidence. Write it down in your booklet.

▶ Over time, the life of the root enters into the grafted branch—the whole thing becomes a new creation. Even after sin separated us from God, our good and true and beautiful Father found a way to graft us back in. God generously offers us his life, his truth, his intimacy. Jesus tells us that our true Father wants to graft us back into his very own family…

▶ This demonstrates why Jesus calls himself the bridegroom and those of us who follow him are the bride: " 'For this reason a man will leave his father and mother and be united to his wife, and the two will become one flesh'? So they are no longer two, but one.

Therefore what God has joined together, let man not separate" (Matthew 19:5-6). **Think how humble God is: At a wedding who receives honor? Who does everyone look at? The bride, of course. God is so humble and kind to us.**

▶ **We've talked a lot about the cut on our branch, but we've said nothing about the cut on the vine—the root that we're grafted into. What's the cut on the vine? The cut in the vine of God happened on the cross—when Jesus was crucified, the vine of God was cut to make it possible for us to be grafted in. It happened brutally, but Jesus submitted himself to the cut because nothing else would allow us to be grafted back in to the vine.**

Let's worship our rescuer, our brother Jesus.

CLOSING WORSHIP (5 MINUTES)

Ask participants to keep their eyes closed as they listen to Chris Tomlin's "Mighty Is the Power of the Cross" (or they can look at the song summary in their booklets on page 50 if they like, or you can get the actual lyrics by going to our Web site at www.pursuitofjesus .com and clicking on the link for them). Then close in prayer. Remember that prayer is conversation, so simply talk to Jesus about the experience you just walked through. This is a great place to thank him for

▶ grafting all of us into his royal family, and giving us the keys to his kingdom.

▶ never giving up in his relentless pursuit to reclaim us from the enemy.

FAMILY MATTERS

▶ **Jesus' Genealogy** (Matthew 1:1-17)—The Bible lists 42 generations from Abraham to David to Joseph to Jesus—42 generations! In your Bible, look at the list of names listed in Jesus' genealogy. What names do you recognize, and what do you know about those people?

▶ **Jesus Stays Behind at the Temple** (Luke 2:41-52)—"Every year [Jesus'] parents went to Jerusalem for the Feast of the Passover. When he was twelve years old, they went up to the Feast, according to the custom. After the Feast was over, while his parents were returning home, the boy Jesus stayed behind in Jerusalem, but they were unaware of it. Thinking he was in their company, they traveled on for a day. Then they began looking for him among their relatives and friends. When they did not find him, they went back to Jerusalem to look for him. After three days they found him in the temple courts, sitting among the teachers, listening to them and asking them questions. Everyone who heard him was amazed at his understanding and his answers. When his parents saw him, they were astonished. His mother said to him, 'Son, why have you treated us like this? Your father and I have been anxiously searching for you.' 'Why were you searching for me?' he asked. 'Didn't you know I had to be in my Father's house?' But they did not understand what he was saying to them. Then he went down to Nazareth with them and was obedient to them. But his mother treasured all these things in her heart. And Jesus grew in wisdom and stature, and in favor with God and men."

▶ **Jesus Turns Water Into Wine for His Mother** (John 2:1-5)—"On the third day a wedding took place at Cana in Galilee. Jesus' mother was there, and Jesus and his disciples had also been invited to the wedding. When the wine was gone, Jesus' mother said to him, 'They have no more wine.' 'Dear woman, why do you involve me?' Jesus replied. 'My time has not yet come.' His mother said to the servants, 'Do whatever he tells you.' "

▶ **The Cost of Following Jesus Includes Family Obligations** (Matthew 8:18-22)—"When Jesus saw the crowd around him, he gave orders to cross to the other side of the lake. Then a teacher of the law came to him and said, 'Teacher, I will follow you wherever you go.' Jesus replied, 'Foxes have holes and birds of the air have nests, but the Son of Man has no place to lay his head.' Another disciple said to him, 'Lord, first let me go and bury my father.' But Jesus told him, 'Follow me, and let the dead bury their own dead.' ''

▶ **Jesus Comes With a Sword, Not Peace** (Matthew 10:34-39)—"Do not suppose that I have come to bring peace to the earth. I did not come to bring peace, but a sword. For I have come to turn 'a man against his father, a daughter against her mother, a daughter-in-law against her mother-in-law—a man's enemies will be the members of his own household.' Anyone who loves his father or mother more than me is not worthy of me; anyone who loves his son or daughter more than me is not worthy of me; and anyone who does not take his cross and follow me is not worthy of me. Whoever finds his life will lose it, and whoever loses his life for my sake will find it."

▶ **Who Are My True Mother and Brothers?** (Matthew 12:46-50)—"While Jesus was still talking to the crowd, his mother and brothers stood outside, wanting to speak to him. Someone told him, 'Your mother and brothers are standing outside, wanting to speak to you.' He replied to him, 'Who is my mother, and who are my brothers?' Pointing to his disciples, he said, 'Here are my mother and my brothers. For whoever does the will of my Father in heaven is my brother and sister and mother.' ''

▶ **Jesus Creates a New Family** (John 19:25-27)—"Near the cross of Jesus stood his mother, his mother's sister, Mary the wife of Clopas, and Mary Magdalene. When Jesus saw his mother there, and the disciple whom he loved standing nearby, he said to his mother, 'Dear woman, here is your son,' and to the disciple, 'Here is your mother.' From that time on, this disciple took her into his home."

"MIGHTY IS THE POWER OF THE CROSS"
BY CHRIS TOMLIN

(Song Summary)

We look for life in so many places—we're desperate for things that will make us feel alive, heal our wounds, take away our blame, fill up our emptiness, and make us whole. But what is powerful enough to do all that?

Well, Jesus' sacrifice—his willing slaughter—on the cross is the only thing powerful enough to do all that.

But, again, we wonder what can rebuild our faith, or show us God's love, or bring us back when we stray, or make our hardened hearts soft again, or release us from the penalty of our own destructive actions? What, really, can save us?

Well, Jesus' sacrifice—his willing slaughter—on the cross is the only thing powerful enough to do all that.

I don't claim to understand this—I just know it's true.

Jesus—only Jesus—is powerful enough to redeem us, and he did it by laying down his power and strength to willingly sacrifice himself on our behalf.

Jesus is our rescuer, our deliverer, our healer, our great Love.

IN PURSUIT OF JESUS

WEEK 6: JESUS AND SATAN'S FAMILY

PRIOR TO THIS SESSION

▶ Set up a boombox or stereo system to play music.

▶ Set up a white board or big pad of paper, along with markers.

▶ Set up a VCR or DVD player connected to a TV or a projector to show a film clip.

▶ Cue up *Amadeus,* Side A, Scene 12, "Absolute Beauty" (55:37–58:35), and set out *The Lion King* (37:40–39:20 and 1:04:10–1:09:15).

WELCOME AND INTRODUCTION (35 MINUTES)

Welcome people to this session.

Then say something like:

All through this series, we've focused not just on Jesus, but on how Jesus related with others in his life. Remember, we're trying to answer Jesus' great question: "Who do you say I am?" So it makes sense to learn about those Jesus related to, because you don't come to know someone in isolation. You watch how that individual interacts with others. So we want to pay attention to Jesus as he engages the people that surround him.

For today's study, we'll target Jesus' relationship with Satan, the enemy of God. Satan is very real. He's actually a fallen angel. And we can learn a lot about Jesus and ourselves by paying attention to his relationship with Satan and the "family" of demons who serve him.

Read aloud John 10:10:

> "The thief comes only to steal and kill and destroy; I have come that they may have life, and have it to the full."

Then read aloud this excerpt from John Eldredge's book *Waking the Dead:*

> "Have you ever wondered why Jesus married those two statements? Did you even know he spoke them at the same time? I mean, he says them in one breath. And he has his reasons. By all means, God intends life for you. But right now that life is *opposed.* It doesn't just roll in on a tray. There is a thief. He comes to steal and kill and destroy. In other words, yes, the offer is life, but you're going to have to fight for it because there's an Enemy in your life with a different agenda. There *is* something set against us."[1]

Then say something like:

> If Satan wants to "steal and kill and destroy" us, we certainly need to understand how Jesus relates to him. Jesus has gone before us to expose this enemy—modeling what it looks like to relate to Satan. Jesus also reveals himself in the light of the enemy.
>
> Let's start by taking inventory of what we know already about Satan. Call out everything you think you know about him, including his many names.

On your white board or pad, write what people call out. You can add any of the following words to the list if no one else does:

- Ruler of this world
- Father of disobedience
- Prowler-devourer-roaring lion
- Schemer
- Deceiver
- Father of lies
- Accuser
- Our adversary
- Evil one

- Under God's authority
- Limited by God in power
- Limited in ability to tempt
- Must obey God and his children
- Limited by time
- God's enemy
- Murderer/thief/destroyer
- Masquerades as Angel of Light

After you finish the list, *ask something like:*

- **What do these familiar names for Satan really mean?**
- **How did Satan become God's enemy?**

THE RULES OF ENGAGEMENT

Whenever you gather input from the whole group—either from a question you ask or as they report back on discussions they have—use these tips to remember how to prime the discussion, ask follow-up questions, and engage the responses you get back:

1. Embrace every answer. Write a condensed version of each one on your white board or pad.
2. If an answer seems vague, confusing, wrong, or sounds like the Sunday school "right" answer, follow up with one of these go-deeper comments or questions:
   - ▶ "Please say more about what you mean."
   - ▶ "I've never thought of that before—could you explain more?"
   - ▶ "That seems to contradict what we commonly believe—could you be more specific?"
   - ▶ "That's the answer we expect. How would you explain that to someone who doesn't know the 'expected' answer?"
3. If an answer is surprising or insightful, ask the person to say a little more (unless the answer was detailed in the first place). You can ask others in the group to expand on that answer, too.
4. When someone specifically connects with where the study is headed, highlight that answer as important to pay attention to.
5. Aim for developing an atmosphere that resembles a good conversation, where you and other group members interact all the time with what someone says.

After you collect a few responses, add these insights if no one else has:

▶ **Revelation 12:7-9 says: "And there was war in heaven. Michael and his angels fought against the dragon, and the dragon and his angels fought back. But he was not strong enough, and they lost their place in heaven. The great dragon was hurled down—that ancient** serpent called the devil, or Satan, who leads the whole world astray. He was hurled to the earth, and his angels with him."

▶ Satan loved his own beauty. He wasn't satisfied with his "place." He's like Absalom, David's son, who wanted to usurp his father's power. First he tried negotiating, and then he rebelled. Absalom didn't just want to dethrone David; he wanted to kill his father. Surprisingly, the story of the prodigal son also contains hints of Satan's story. He ended up as an outcast outside his father's kingdom, but wasn't destroyed. What if the prodigal had responded with rage instead of repentance? He would've been the passionate enemy of his father.

▶ Satan is now defeated. He can no longer directly assault God. But because he desperately wants to hurt God any way he can, Satan turns his attention to God's children. Revelation 12:13 says, "When the dragon saw that he had been hurled to the earth, he pursued the woman who had given birth to the male child."

SHOW FILM CLIP

Say something like:

Because God has defeated Satan, we struggle to understand what motivates Satan now. A film clip can help us. In the film *Amadeus*, Salieri, the emperor's court composer in Vienna, slowly goes insane because of his jealousy for Mozart's incredible musical gifts. In this scene, Mozart's wife secretly (and innocently) brings Salieri some original copies of music Mozart has been working on—hoping Salieri will think the music is good enough to buy. Salieri is overcome with disgust for the beauty Mozart has created.

Show the scene from *Amadeus*. The clip on the DVD is from Side A, Scene 12, "Absolute Beauty" (55:37–58:35).

After the clip, *ask something like:*

▶ **What parallels do you see between Salieri and Satan?**

Remember to use The Rules of Engagement. After you gather a few responses, *say something like:*

Now that we have a better idea of what motivates Satan, let's focus on how he lives out his hatred. Again, let's explore that question by watching a scene from a film.

SHOW FILM CLIP

Say something like:

In the animated film *The Lion King,* Mufasa, the lion king of all the animals, is trampled to death in a stampede while rushing to save the life of his son, Simba. After Simba discovers his father's lifeless body, his evil uncle Scar lies to him about his father's death—a death Scar actually orchestrated. But Scar tells Simba that he actually caused his own father's death.

Show the scene from *The Lion King*, from 37:40–39:20.

After the clip, *ask something like:*

▶ **What lies does Scar tell Simba? How do these reflect the lies Satan tells us?**

Remember to use The Rules of Engagement. After you gather many responses, add these insights if no one else has:

▶ **Scar lies to Simba by telling him, essentially: "You're to blame for your father's death. What's more, you've done this before. Your mother will be ashamed of you, even reject you. You'd better run away and never return."**

▶ By telling us our heart is bad and that we'll never be acceptable to God, Satan keeps us from returning to our true family with God. He lies about our Father, and he lies about us.

▶ Satan's lies affect us in two ways:

1. His lies shame us, making us feel as if we're intrinsically bad. This affects how we see ourselves. We won't return "home" to God if Satan convinces us that God will reject us.

2. Satan's lies undermine our trust in Jesus, and thus our ability to be intimate with him. This affects how we see God. We won't return "home" to God if we think we can't trust him.

Ask something like:

▶ If nothing changes in Simba's story, how will this lie eventually affect him? What's the impact of Satan's lies in our lives?

Remember to use The Rules of Engagement.

JESUS INTERACTING WITH SATAN (30 MINUTES)

After you gather responses and add your own insights, *say something like:*

Now let's look more closely at Jesus' relationship with Satan. We want to discover how Jesus intends to counteract Satan's assault on us, and how Jesus reveals his own goodness and trustworthiness to us. In 1 John 3:8, the apostle says Jesus appeared for this purpose—"to destroy the devil's work."

Maybe we can find some clues about how Jesus intends to destroy the devil's work by taking a closer look at Satan's temptation of Jesus in the wilderness.

Read aloud Matthew 4:1-11 (from *The Message*) while participants follow along in their booklets:

"Next Jesus was taken into the wild by the Spirit for the Test. The Devil was ready to give it. Jesus prepared for the Test by fasting forty days and forty nights. That left him, of course, in a state of extreme hunger, which the Devil took advantage of in the first test: 'Since you are God's Son, speak the word that will turn these stones into loaves of bread.'

"Jesus answered by quoting Deuteronomy: 'It takes more than bread to stay alive. It takes a steady stream of words from God's mouth.'

"For the second test the Devil took him to the Holy City. He sat him on top of the Temple and said, 'Since you are God's Son, jump.' The Devil goaded him by quoting Psalm 91: 'He has placed you in the care of angels. They will catch you so that you won't so much as stub your toe on a stone.'

"Jesus countered with another citation from Deuteronomy: 'Don't you dare test the Lord your God.'

"For the third test, the Devil took him to the peak of a huge mountain. He gestured expansively, pointing out all the earth's kingdoms, how glorious they all were. Then he said, 'They're yours—lock, stock, and barrel. Just go down on your knees and worship me, and they're yours.'

"Jesus' refusal was curt: 'Beat it, Satan!' He backed his rebuke with a third quotation from Deuteronomy: 'Worship the Lord your God, and only him. Serve him with absolute single-heartedness.'

"The Test was over. The Devil left. And in his place, angels! Angels came and took care of Jesus' needs."

Ask something like:

▶ What different ways did Satan try to attack and destroy Jesus in the wilderness?

Remember to use The Rules of Engagement. After people offer answers to the question, add these insights if no one else has:

- ▶ Satan tried to call Jesus' true identity into question—just as he does with us.
- ▶ Satan invited Jesus to satisfy his hunger with something other than God. The truth is that Jesus satisfies us—that's why he calls himself "the bread of life" and "living water."
- ▶ Satan goaded Jesus to accept power and authority not given by God. Jesus already possesses "all authority" by his Father; he doesn't need any more.
- ▶ Satan tried to seduce Jesus into worshipping someone other than God. He also offers us many other "easier" false gods to worship—money, fame, ego, power, consumption, and on and on.
- ▶ Satan challenged Jesus to test God to see if he's really good. Satan put this same "test" before Adam and Eve. This is why Jesus is called "the new Adam." He reaffirms the goodness of God.

Then ask something like:

- ▶ Why would Satan attack Jesus in these specific ways?
- ▶ What assumptions does Satan make about why Jesus has come?
- ▶ What assumptions does Satan make about Jesus' heart?

After several participants answer, add these insights if no one else has:

- ▶ Satan believes Jesus isn't really any better, smarter, or more powerful than he is.
- ▶ Satan believes he can corrupt Jesus by telling lies about God; after all, it worked with Adam and Eve.
- ▶ Satan believes Jesus came to earth to gather power and authority for himself, just as Satan did when God cast him out of heaven.

Then ask these follow-up questions:

- ▶ Why did Jesus respond to Satan the way he did?
- ▶ Jesus used Scripture to respond. Why?
- ▶ Unlike his interactions with the Pharisees, Jesus never raised his voice or got angry or called Satan names. Why?

If no one mentions this insight, add it to the mix:

Maybe Jesus spoke harshly to the Pharisees because they still had hope. Everything Jesus does, even using harsh words and anger, is motivated by love. He loved the Pharisees, and perhaps he targeted his harsh words at upsetting them enough to reconsider the deadly path they were on.

On the other hand, Satan has no hope. The Bible clearly says that he's headed for eternal destruction. Maybe Jesus didn't speak harshly to Satan because it wouldn't help him at all.

Remember to follow The Rules of Engagement. After you hear responses from participants, *say something like:*

Later, Jesus spent much of his ministry time casting out demons from oppressed and possessed people and rebuking Satan and his "family."

If you like, and you have time, you can give some examples by referencing the "Jesus Destroying the Works of Satan" box on page 110. Participants can also find these in their booklets on page 55.

Ask something like:

- ▶ What can we learn about responding to Satan's influence in our lives from the way Jesus responded to Satan and his "family"?

▶ What does Jesus want to communicate about himself with his actions?

Remember to use The Rules of Engagement. After many participants answer, be sure to add this insight if no one else has:

Jesus tries to communicate this to us: "I'm good. I'm stronger than Satan. I'm God. I have all the authority. I'm trustworthy. I'm not intimidated or tricked by Satan's lies. Because of me, you don't have to live under the influence of Satan and his lies."

CLOSING CELEBRATION (15 MINUTES)

Ask people to close their eyes.

Say something like:

Whether or not we acknowledge it, we all fight a spiritual battle with the enemy of God. Satan always desires to destroy us by destroying our own true identity and God's true identity. His tactics and his lies never change over time.

Ask participants to ponder these questions quietly. Pause between each question to give people silent time to consider each one:

▶ As you think about your life right now, where do you see Satan harassing you with his tactics and lies?

▶ Are the lies about you, about God, or about both?

▶ Do you believe that God is good in every instance and circumstance?

▶ Do you trust God in all his dealings with you?

▶ Are you convinced of God's overarching power and authority?

▶ Do you believe with certainty that God has the ability to fill up your hunger and thirst with himself?

▶ Have you rejected shame and blame in your life, not allowing it to take root?

Say something like:

In the end, if we answer "no" to any of these questions, we unwittingly sign on to Satan's lies. We subconsciously conspire with him.

Yet, we have a path to freedom—a strategy for clinging to the truth while rejecting Satan's lies. The path always involves remembering who Jesus really is—answering the question: "Who do you say I am?"

SHOW FILM CLIP

Say something like:

Let's close by watching how Simba found that path.

Show the scene where Rafiki, the wise baboon, meets Simba in the wilderness and tells him, "I know who you are." Rafiki leads Simba to a pool, where the young lion encounters the image of his father Mufasa. Mufasa's advice to Simba is to remember him and to remember who he really is. Simba then goes back to the Prideland and assumes his rightful identity as king. Show the scene from *The Lion King*—1:04:10–1:09:15 on the DVD.

Close in prayer, emphasizing these truths:
▶ It's crucial that we remember Jesus as he really is—that we don't forget him.
▶ In the light of Jesus, we also need to remember who we are—true brothers and sisters of Jesus, and children of our good Father.

JESUS DESTROYING THE WORKS OF SATAN

- ▶ Jesus is mocked and "outed" by a demon, but he muzzles the demon (Luke 4:33-35).
- ▶ Jesus casts demons out of "many" early in ministry (Luke 4:41).
- ▶ Jesus casts a "mob" of demons out of Gerasene man (Luke 8:26-36).
- ▶ Jesus casts out a demon from a possessed boy (Luke 9:38-43).
- ▶ Jesus' disciples say, "Even the demons are subject to us!" (Luke 10:17-20, NAS).
- ▶ Jesus tells Peter, "Get behind me, Satan!...You are not setting your mind on God's interests, but man's" (Matthew 16:23, NAS).
- ▶ The Pharisees accuse Jesus of using Satan's power to exorcise (Luke 11:14-26).
- ▶ Jesus casts out a demon from a woman on the Sabbath (Luke 13:10-16).
- ▶ Jesus allows Satan to "sift" Peter (Luke 22:31-34). Satan demands permission, and God gives Satan room to move against Peter, but only for God's greater purposes in Peter's life. Satan is constrained, just as he was constrained in his attacks on Job.

ENDNOTE 1: John Eldredge, *Waking the Dead: The Glory of a Heart Fully Alive* (Thomas Nelson, 2003), p. 13.

WEEK 7: JESUS AND HIS TRUE MISSION

PRIOR TO THIS SESSION

- ▶ Set up a boombox or stereo system to play music.
- ▶ Set up a white board or big pad of paper, along with markers.
- ▶ Set up a VCR or DVD player connected to a TV or a projector to show a film clip.
- ▶ Cue up track 11, "Why It Matters," on Sara Groves' *Add to the Beauty* CD for your opening worship.
- ▶ Set out Michael Card's *The Life* CD for your closing worship. You'll play track 10, "Jesus Let Us Come to Know You," at that time.
- ▶ Cue up the first of two successive scenes you'll show from the 1998 film *Les Misérables* (29:20–41:00 and 45:48–47:05 on the DVD).

WELCOME AND INTRODUCTION (10 MINUTES)

Welcome people as they arrive. Then direct them to the song summary of the Sara Groves song "Why It Matters" on page 59 in their booklets (or you can get the actual lyrics to the song by going to the link on our Web site at www.pursuitofjesus.com). Play the song, and ask participants to listen as they read the summary.

After the song, instruct people to find a partner to discuss these questions:

- ▶ **What do the words "protest of the darkness" mean in this song? How might Jesus be a "protest of the darkness"?**

After a few minutes, ask a few people to summarize their answers. Then ask the whole group to respond to this question:

▶ **What do we really know about Jesus' true mission on earth?**

For this question, write participants' answers on the lower part of your white board or pad. Leave the top half empty.

THE RULES OF ENGAGEMENT

Whenever you gather input from the whole group—either from a question you ask or as they report back on discussions they have—use these tips to remember how to prime the discussion, ask follow-up questions, and engage the responses you get back:

1. Embrace every answer. Write a condensed version of each one on your white board or pad.
2. If an answer seems vague, confusing, wrong, or sounds like the Sunday school "right" answer, follow up with one of these go-deeper comments or questions:
   ▶ "Please say more about what you mean."
   ▶ "I've never thought of that before—could you explain more?"
   ▶ "That seems to contradict what we commonly believe—could you be more specific?"
   ▶ "That's the answer we expect. How would you explain that to someone who doesn't know the 'expected' answer?"
3. If an answer is surprising or insightful, ask the person to say a little more (unless the answer was detailed in the first place). You can ask others in the group to expand on that answer, too.
4. When someone specifically connects with where the study is headed, highlight that answer as important to pay attention to.
5. Aim for developing an atmosphere that resembles a good conversation, where you and other group members interact all the time with what someone says.

After you collect many responses, *say something like:*

These answers are all true, scriptural, and rich with meaning. Yet, we're after something even bigger. Let's collect these answers under a small umbrella. *(Draw a curved line over the answers you've written, so it looks like an umbrella.)*

The big question that remains for us to explore is not "What?" but "Why?" Let's explore the "Why?" behind Jesus' mission, and we'll leave space above our initial answers to write what we learn. *(Draw another curved line at the top of your white board or pad.)* However, I don't think we'll find what we're looking for simply by covering the same ground the same way.

EXPLORE JESUS THROUGH STORY (60 MINUTES)

Say something like:

In the last hundred years, we've radically changed the way we look at Scripture. Because of the industrial revolution and the rise of science as our primary (and often only) gauge of truth, we naturally use and respect scientific practices and habits to prove God and his truths. For example, "absolute truth" is a science-based term.

Dr. Francis S. Collins, the director of the Human Genome Project, says: "I had to admit that the science I loved so much was powerless to answer questions such as 'What is the meaning of life?' 'Why am I here?' 'Why does mathematics work, anyway?' 'If the universe had a beginning, who created it?'…'Why do humans have a moral sense?' 'What happens after we die?' "[1]

We're most familiar with pursuing Jesus through propositional truths. Proposition means, literally, a "statement that affirms or denies something." So a propositional truth is simply a statement about truth. A biblical example that's often used is: "For all have sinned and fall short of the glory of God" (Romans 3:23). Essentially, we tear apart the larger story of the gospel so we can break it into lists and statements of what we should and shouldn't do as Christians.

When we approach the story of Jesus propositionally, we do find truths—with a small t. But this propositional approach does not, by itself, get at the Truth with a capital T. Because we approach Scripture mostly propositionally, we put the Bible alongside every other work of proposition that claims to have answers for living well and true. But the Bible isn't written propositionally. Rather, Scripture is written as a collection of stories that ultimately point to Jesus.

Bible scholars agree that the gripping story in the book of Job was the first portion of the Bible ever written. Generally, they believe Moses wrote the book of Job before Genesis. And the gripping story in the book of Hosea was the first written by "the writing prophets." The commentaries say, "Hosea believed that it is important to know God as a person."

Donald Miller, popular Christian author of the best seller *Blue Like Jazz*, tried to address the tension between propositional truth and "story truth" when he explained on his Web site why he wrote his sequel to *Blue Like Jazz*, the book *Searching for God Knows What*. Let's listen...

Read aloud Donald Miller's explanation for why he wrote the book *Searching for God Knows What*. Tell participants they can follow along on page 57 in their booklets:

"I wrapped this book up [on a] night I felt like I was losing it a bit. Essentially, I had begun to wonder if I had misunderstood the gospel of Jesus, thinking of it in propositional terms rather than relational dynamics. The latter seemed too poetic to be true, but the former had been killing my soul for years and was simply illogical. If we hold that Jesus wanted us to 'believe' certain ideas or 'do' certain things in order to be a Christian, we are holding to heresy...I finished the last paragraph and felt a kind of sickness at the thought of whether or not I was telling the truth. But after further consideration, and after re-writing the book, I realized the formulaic version of Christianity was irrational, and for that matter, unbiblical. True Christian spirituality mirrors relational dynamics more than the workings of a free-market economy. This seemed to open up an entire new world to me, a world where every thought and feeling operates as a kind of living meta-phor for the workings of the Godhead.

"As a year has passed since the release of the book, I've seen more and more how, in my own life and in the lives of the Christians around me, we subscribe to false gospels that are troubling our souls. Because we live in a constant sales environment where we are told a certain car will make us sexy or a certain dishwashing detergent will be a miracle for our dishes, we assume the gospel of Jesus works the same way, that is, if we invest something, we get something more back. But this is not the case. To understand what the Bible explains Jesus' gospel to be, we must look to each other, to the way a father interacts with a child, a bride to a bridegroom, a doctor to a patient. When we let go of the idea of Jesus as a product and embrace Him as a being, our path to spiritual maturity begins."[2]

Say something like:

Let's explore the answer to our question—What is Jesus' true mis-sion?—by diving into a story. Remember that God reveals himself to us through the collections of stories that make up the Bible.

For our exploration, we'll look at part of a story written by Victor Hugo in 1862—*Les Misérables*. His story was made into a successful Broadway musical and, later, a successful film starring Liam Neeson, Uma Thurman, and Geoffrey Rush. Unlike other times in this pursuit, we'll watch a much longer portion of the story—almost 15 minutes. While this story is raw, you'll also sense a real beauty in it. And you should see many clues to Jesus' true mission in this story. We'll stop the story briefly to skip over a brutal portion.

SHOW FILM CLIP

Say something like:

The 1998 film version of *Les Misérables* follows the story of ex-convict Jean Valjean, a man imprisoned in France to 19 years of hard labor for stealing a loaf of bread for his hungry family. Valjean gains his release from prison, but he can't get a job because he's an ex-convict. He resorts to stealing from a kind bishop who invites him into his home. Valjean injures the bishop when he's caught stealing. In a powerful scene, the bishop keeps Valjean from going to jail—literally, the bishop redeems Valjean and challenges him to live his life for God.

From that point on, Valjean lives passionately for God and for the poor and oppressed. He becomes a successful businessman and political leader. When, without Valjean's knowledge, one of his factory workers is wrongfully fired from her job at his factory, she descends into poverty and prostitution and bitterness toward Valjean, because she believes he ordered her firing. In this long scene you'll see Fantine, the young woman, struggle to stay alive on the street just before she meets Valjean again. Just a warning that this scene contains some rough language near the beginning.

Play the back-to-back clips from *Les Misérables* that chronicle the relationship between Fantine and Jean Valjean (29:20–41:00, then 45:48–47:05). Make sure to stop the DVD after the first segment and fast-forward to the second segment—the gap between the segments has some scenes that are hard to watch and aren't crucial for this discussion. Also, early on in the scene, some rough and drunken men interact with Fantine and use coarse language. You can lower the volume on this portion if your group might be offended by this language.

After the successive film clips, *ask these questions:*

▶ **What makes it difficult for Fantine to trust that Valjean wants to offer her a pure love?**

▶ **What must happen in Fantine, the prostitute, to allow Valjean to love her?**

▶ **What obstacles must Valjean overcome to convince Fantine to receive real love from him?**

▶ **What does Valjean do to convince Fantine to be loved by him? to woo her?**

Follow The Rules of Engagement. After you collect many responses to the questions, if no one else offers this insight, add it into the mix:

Jean Valjean shows Fantine his true heart, over and over. He never pushes himself on her, and never expects or requires love back. But slowly, over time, love wins Fantine's trust. Valjean's last kiss on her forehead, which passes over her lips, is a beautiful act of love that's pure. He isn't intent on using her.

Remind everyone that you're trying to get at the question of Jesus' true mission through the lens of story. Then ask people to respond to this question to connect the story of Valjean and Fantine to the story of Jesus and us:

▶ **If we treat Valjean as a symbol for Christ and Fantine as a symbol for us, what can we learn about Jesus' true mission on earth from this story?**

Use The Rules of Engagement. After you collect and prod many responses, if no one offers these insights, add them to the mix:

- ▶ Jesus said, "You are my bride *(my beloved)*, and I am the bridegroom." In fact, he repeatedly refers to himself as the Bridegroom and describes us repeatedly as the Bride. In Matthew 25, for example, Jesus tells the parable of the Bridegroom. In Revelation 19:7, he tells the story of the wedding feast of the Lamb. In Romans 7, Paul describes our redemption by Christ in terms of divorce and remarriage.

- ▶ The Bride *(who is us)* is the gatekeeper for intimacy. She must choose to receive and yield herself to the Bridegroom. Ultimately she *allows* the Bridegroom a deeper level of intimacy. Without her permission and yielding, it is rape.

- ▶ But the Bride continually seeks other lovers. The Bible says that "while we were still sinners, Christ died for us" and "we love because he first loved us." In the early part of Romans, Paul says we are all without excuse for our sin. We're all caught under the umbrella of sin. In Romans 7, Paul dramatically says, "What a wretched man I am! Who will rescue me from this body of death? Thanks be to God—through Jesus Christ our Lord!" Jesus the Bridegroom is our rescuer.

- ▶ The true mission of Jesus Christ is to reunite the Bride with the Bridegroom—to woo us and show us his true nature, so that (like Fantine) we can overcome our distrust of him, and our own shame, and give ourselves to him freely.

After the discussion, *say something like:*

This explains so many things that seem hard about Jesus. For example:

- ▶ Think about the story of the rich young ruler. Why does Jesus require everything of him? The answer is that Jesus wants intimacy, and he won't settle for a "marriage of convenience." He loves with abandon, and he longs for the same from us.

▶ Think about Jesus telling us that we must "eat the flesh of the Son of Man and drink his blood" to have any part of him. That's so intimate it scares us.

▶ Think about Jesus telling us we must "hate" our father and mother or we're not worthy of him. That sounds so harsh. But when a man and woman get married, they leave their fathers and mothers to be joined to their beloved.

Jesus spelled all of this out clearly in what we call the High Priestly Prayer, in John 17.

Read aloud John 17:1-12, 20-26 from *The Message* (see page 121). Tell participants they can follow along in their booklets on page 60. If you're tight on time going into the closing, simply tell participants to read Jesus' prayer on their own sometime during the upcoming week.

CLOSING WORSHIP (5 MINUTES)

Say something like:

Have you ever considered why God didn't just kill Satan and his angels? Instead, God threw Satan to earth. A dictator would just kill his defeated enemies.

God is so much better than a dictator. But how often do we think of God as being a dictator? It comes down to this: God wants us to have the freedom to choose him, so he sent his Son to woo us, to show us himself, to kiss us on our foreheads, to invite us into intimacy. He passionately hopes that we will love him back.

Let's close now by worshipping him as we listen to this song by Michael Card.

Play the Michael Card song "Jesus Let Us Come to Know You." Then close in prayer. Remember that prayer is conversation, so simply talk to Jesus about the experience you just walked through. This is a great place to thank him for

- ▶ rescuing us forever from the enemy's wicked plans to destroy us.
- ▶ not just inviting us to his wedding, but making us his bride!

"WHY IT MATTERS" BY SARA GROVES
(Song Summary)

I need to hear the story of God's redemptive love again—it's so easy for me to forget it all. Not because I literally forget it, but because I know it so well that I take it for granted. I forget how beautiful, and how powerful, God's story really is.

Remind me again of why our paltry little efforts to reflect the goodness of that story still matter so much—remind me again of how important it is to tell others of the beauty of God's story.

In the midst of terror and hardship and tragedy, we must remind ourselves of the greater truth—of the real and present beauty of God's love for us. When we do, it's our way of protesting the lies and destruction of God's enemy.

It's the little acts of love and beauty that really matter—that remind us of God's greater acts of love and beauty. We need these tiny acts of beauty like we need little footholds on a sheer cliff. Sometimes all we need is a tiny, solid foothold to keep us from falling.

ENDNOTE 1: Excerpted from an article on CNN.com by Dr. Francis Collins, "Collins: Why This Scientist Believes in God."

ENDNOTE 2: From Donald Miller's explanation of why he wrote *Searching for God Knows What*, on his Web site www .donaldmillerwords.com.

JESUS' HIGH PRIESTLY PRAYER

John 17:1-12, 20-26 (The Message)

Jesus said these things. Then, raising his eyes in prayer, he said:
Father, it's time.
Display the bright splendor of your Son
So the Son in turn may show your bright splendor.
You put him in charge of everything human
So he might give real and eternal life to all in his charge.
And this is the real and eternal life:
That they know you,
The one and only true God,
And Jesus Christ, whom you sent.
I glorified you on earth
By completing down to the last detail
What you assigned me to do.
And now, Father, glorify me with your very own splendor,
The very splendor I had in your presence
Before there was a world.
I spelled out your character in detail
To the men and women you gave me.
They were yours in the first place;
Then you gave them to me,
And they have now done what you said.
They know now, beyond the shadow of a doubt,
That everything you gave me is firsthand from you,
For the message you gave me, I gave them;
And they took it, and were convinced
That I came from you.
They believed that you sent me.

I pray for them.
I'm not praying for the God-rejecting world
But for those you gave me,
For they are yours by right.
Everything mine is yours, and yours mine,
And my life is on display in them.
For I'm no longer going to be visible in the world;
They'll continue in the world
While I return to you.
Holy Father, guard them as they pursue this life
That you conferred as a gift through me,
So they can be one heart and mind
As we are one heart and mind.
As long as I was with them, I guarded them
In the pursuit of the life you gave through me;
I even posted a night watch.
And not one of them got away,
Except for the rebel bent on destruction
(the exception that proved the rule of Scripture).
I'm praying not only for them
But also for those who will believe in me
Because of them and their witness about me.
The goal is for all of them to become one heart and mind—
Just as you, Father, are in me and I in you,
So they might be one heart and mind with us.
Then the world might believe that you, in fact, sent me.
The same glory you gave me, I gave them,
So they'll be as unified and together as we are—
I in them and you in me.

Then they'll be mature in this oneness,
And give the godless world evidence
That you've sent me and loved them
In the same way you've loved me.
Father, I want those you gave me
To be with me, right where I am,
So they can see my glory, the splendor you gave me,
Having loved me
Long before there ever was a world.
Righteous Father, the world has never known you,
But I have known you, and these disciples know
That you sent me on this mission.
I have made your very being known to them—
Who you are and what you do—
And continue to make it known,
So that your love for me
Might be in them
Exactly as I am in them.

IN PURSUIT OF JESUS

WEEK 8: JESUS ACTING SUPERNATURALLY

PRIOR TO THIS SESSION

▶ Set up a boombox or stereo system to play music.

▶ Set up a white board or big pad of paper, along with markers.

▶ Set up a VCR or DVD player connected to a TV or a projector to show a film clip.

▶ Cue up track 3, "Serve Hymn/Holy Is the Lord" on Andrew Peterson's *Love and Thunder* CD for your closing worship.

▶ Cue up the train scene from *Spiderman 2* (1:36:50–1:41:35 on the DVD).

WELCOME AND INTRODUCTION (25 MINUTES)

Welcome participants to the session, *then say something like:*

I'd like everyone to stand up and find a partner who's roughly your size. The person with the longest arm should go first in this activity.

Face each other at arm's length. Partner 1, you'll hold your right arm straight out in front of you at a 90-degree angle from your body (demonstrate for them). Partner 2, you'll use your left arm to try to push down on top of your partner's arm with firm but gentle pressure. Partner 1, you'll try to keep your arm from going down while repeating, "My name is (your name)." Repeat this over and over while your partner attempts to push your arm down. We'll do this for about 10 seconds. Go!

Most often the arm won't go down, unless there's a big size or strength difference in partners. Now have partners do the same activity all over again, but this time the first person should repeatedly say, "My name is Bart Simpson" instead of his or her real name. This time, the arm typically will go down.

Have partners switch roles and do the activity again, so each one can experience the unusual effect. It's OK if this doesn't "work" with everyone. But it works most of the time, and people will generally be amazed by it.

After the activity, tell people they can be seated.

Ask something like:

If your arm went down when you said, "My name is Bart Simpson," answer this question: How is what happened to you like or unlike a supernatural experience?

THE RULES OF ENGAGEMENT

Whenever you gather input from the whole group—either from a question you ask or as they report back on discussions they have—use these tips to remember how to prime the discussion, ask follow-up questions, and engage the responses you get back:

1. Embrace every answer. Write a condensed version of each one on your white board or pad.
2. If an answer seems vague, confusing, wrong, or sounds like the Sunday school "right" answer, follow up with one of these go-deeper comments or questions:
   ▶ "Please say more about what you mean."
   ▶ "I've never thought of that before—could you explain more?"
   ▶ "That seems to contradict what we commonly believe—could you be more specific?"
   ▶ "That's the answer we expect. How would you explain that to someone who doesn't know the 'expected' answer?"
3. If an answer is surprising or insightful, ask the person to say a little more (unless the answer was detailed in the first place). You can ask others in the group to expand on that answer, too.
4. When someone specifically connects with where the study is headed, highlight that answer as important to pay attention to.
5. Aim for developing an atmosphere that resembles a good conversation, where you and other group members interact all the time with what someone says.

After you gather feedback from the question, *say something like:*

The effect many of you experienced is likely tied to a powerful neurological truth—the same phenomenon measured by a lie detector test. Because you're not telling the truth the second time you try to hold your arm up, your brain changes your physical response.

SHOW FILM CLIP

Say something like:

You know, the closest many of us get to a real miracle is when we watch a movie about a superhero. Let's watch this scene from *Spiderman 2*. In it, Spiderman fights his archenemy Doc Ock, who has sabotaged a hurtling train. All of the passengers on the train will die unless Spiderman can save them.

Play the clip from *Spiderman 2* (1:36:50–1:41:35).

Ask something like:

▶ **What emotions did you feel toward Spiderman as you watched this clip? In your booklet list all the emotions you felt as you watched— just write words that represent your emotions.**

After a couple of minutes, ask participants to tell you what they wrote. *Then say something like:*

Interestingly, none of us wrote the word "fear." Maybe we were scared *for* Spiderman, but we weren't afraid *of* him—even though he clearly has the power and ability to further harm the people on the train. (In the highly unlikely event that someone mentions being afraid *of* Spiderman—not afraid *for* him—simply change this response to: Interestingly, only one of us wrote the word "fear.")

Ask something like:

▶ **Why do you think we're oblivious to Spiderman's ability to intentionally harm the people on the train?**

Remember to follow The Rules of Engagement. After you gather a few responses, if someone doesn't offer this insight, add it to the mix:

We're convinced of Spiderman's good intentions, aren't we? Even more, we're convinced that he's good. It would be out of character, and somehow deeply disappointing, if Spiderman suddenly acted in a mean or evil way with people in trouble.

Next, highlight a story told by Mark Galli, a former pastor and an associate editor for Christianity Today. Read aloud the story of Galli's encounter with a Laotian family from his book *Jesus Mean and Wild:*

Say something like:

Galli was pastoring a church in Sacramento when a group of refugees from Laos asked him how they could become members of the church. They were new to the church and were attending because the congregation had sponsored their relocation to Sacramento. They knew little of Christianity, so Galli suggested they do a Bible study focusing on the book of Mark. The Laotians agreed, and Galli dived into the study with them. Here's Galli's account of what happened next, from the book *Jesus Mean and Wild*:

"After we read the passage in which Jesus calms the storm, I began as I usually did with more theologically sophisticated groups: I asked them about the storms in their lives. There was a puzzled look among my Laotian friends, so I elaborated: we all have storms—problems, worries, troubles, crises—and this story teaches that Jesus can give us peace in the midst of those storms. 'So what are your storms?' I asked.

"Again, more puzzled silence. Finally, one of the men hesitantly asked, 'Do you mean that Jesus actually calmed the wind and sea in the middle of a storm?'

"I thought he was finding the story incredulous, and I didn't want to get distracted with the problem of miracles. So I replied, 'Yes, but we should not get hung up on the details of the miracle. We should remember that Jesus can calm the storms in our lives.'

"Another stretch of awkward silence ensued until another replied, 'Well, if Jesus calmed the wind and the waves, he must be a very power-ful man!' At this, they all nodded vigorously and chattered excitedly to one another in Lao. Except for me, the room was full of awe and wonder.

"I suddenly realized that they grasped the story better than I did, and I finally acknowledged, 'Yes, Jesus is a very powerful person. In fact, Christians believe he is the Creator of heaven and earth, and thus, of course, he has power over the wind and the waves.' "[1]

Ask something like:

If we're honest, we're a lot like Mark Galli. Why do we so often struggle to believe in the literal power of Jesus in our lives?

Remember to use The Rules of Engagement.

THE EXTRAVAGANCE OF JESUS' SUPERNATURAL ACTS (40 MINUTES)

Briefly remind people about the story of Jesus calming the storm while the frightened disciples huddled on the boat together (from Matthew 8:23-27).

Then say something like:

> Sometimes Jesus performed supernatural feats that had nothing to do with healing people or casting out demons. These miracles almost reflect what we might see in a Spiderman film. For example:
>
> ▶ Jesus changes water into wine at the Cana wedding (John 2:1-11).
> ▶ Jesus commands a miraculous catch of fish for the first disciples (Luke 5:4-9).
> ▶ Jesus calls Nathanael by telling him he "saw" Nathanael when he was too far away to see (John 1:43-49).
> ▶ Jesus seems to know the thoughts of others (Matthew 9:1-4).
> ▶ Jesus feeds the 5,000 with a few loaves and fish (Matthew 14:15-21).
> ▶ Jesus walks on the sea in full view of his disciples (Matthew 14:22-33).
> ▶ Jesus feeds the 4,000 with a few loaves and fish (Matthew 15:32-38).
> ▶ Jesus curses the fig tree, and it withers on the spot (Matthew 21:18-20).
>
> Let's explore what Jesus wants us to know about him—and about his Father—through these supernatural acts. We'll do this by diving into some questions about Jesus' supernatural acts.

Instruct people to get with two others to form a trio, then assign each trio one of the "Supernatural Jesus Questions" (on page 65) to pursue.

Before they start, *say something like:*

> Remember the habits of our pursuit—our tasting skills. Slow down, fuel your curiosity, pay attention to details, and ask more

questions. Together, as a trio, I want you to come up with a detailed answer to your question. You're welcome to refer to the Bible story referenced in each question if you want.

Play unobtrusive instrumental music in the background as people discuss their questions.

SUPERNATURAL JESUS QUESTIONS:[2]

- ▶ If Jesus could walk on water, why didn't he ever fly? (John 6:15-21)
- ▶ Jesus' first recorded miracle was turning the water into wine at a wedding feast in Cana. This almost seems like a party trick rather than an appropriate use of his authority and ability, so why did he do it? (John 2:1-11)
- ▶ Twice Jesus fed a huge crowd with just a few loaves and some fish. Why didn't Jesus produce food in this way for every meal he ate? (Matthew 14:13-21)
- ▶ If Jesus had played sports, would he have been good enough to compete in the Olympics? Why or why not? (John 6:19)
- ▶ Do you think Jesus really knew the hidden thoughts of people, or did he have no more knowledge of others than we do? Explain. (Matthew 9:1-4)
- ▶ Did Jesus need to learn how to read or how to do math, or did he just know these things intrinsically? Explain. (John 16:30)
- ▶ At one point, Jesus tells Nathanael that he could see Nathanael sitting under a fig tree before he'd ever met him—a supernatural feat. Did Jesus have "superpowers" like a comic book hero? If so, what were they? If not, how do you explain his ability to see someone too far away to see? (John 1:43-51)

After five or six minutes, ask a spokesperson from each trio to summarize their answer to the assigned question. After each summary, ask the rest of the participants to push back against, affirm, add to, and clarify what they hear, and you should do the same. Remember to use The Rules of Engagement. These questions might help you specifically spur this conversation further:

- Do I really understand or agree with the answer?
- Did the answer include words or descriptions that need to be explored further?
- Did the answer contradict what we already know about Jesus?
- Did the answer connect to something else we know about Jesus?

After you hear and engage with each trio's responses, *say something like:*

Award-winning author Annie Dillard once wrote: "On the whole, I do not find Christians, outside of the catacombs, sufficiently sensible of the conditions. Does anyone have the foggiest idea of what sort of power we so blithely invoke? Or, as I suspect, does no one believe a word of it?"[3]

Then ask something like:

- Dillard targets a big issue for us—whether we *really* believe in the power of God. When the paralytic in John 5:1-9—who had camped out by the pool of Bethsaida for many years hoping to be healed—asked Jesus to heal him, why did Jesus *first* ask him if he really wanted to be healed?

Gather responses and follow The Rules of Engagement.
If no one offers this insight, add it to the mix:

Maybe Annie Dillard pinpointed one of our great struggles as Christians: We really don't believe. Why? Well, maybe we still think we can be like gods and take care of things ourselves. Maybe a Jesus this powerful scares us—we're scared both of what he will do and what he won't do. Maybe we're afraid that faith is just a fairy tale, so we doubt if we should really invest our hearts in it.

Now read aloud the end of the Mark Galli story from *Jesus Mean and Wild*:

> "This simplistic answer [of Mark Galli to the Laotians' question about Jesus' power] would not have gone over in some of the more sophisticated congregations of which I've been a part. As I noted, it didn't go over with me until I was confronted with my unbelief. The reasons for that are complex, but I think one is that the power of Christ frightens us—as well it should. And we'll do anything to avoid facing it as an ongoing reality, much to our loss."[4]

CLOSING MEDITATION (10 MINUTES)

Ask people to close their eyes, then have them ask God this question and journal what they "hear":

> **God, am I frightened by your power? If so, why? If not, why not?**

To close the session, invite participants to journal in their booklets any response they sense from God. Tell them you'll give them an uncomfortably long silence to "listen" for God's answer to the questions. After four or five minutes, play the song "Serve Hymn/ Holy Is the Lord" from Andrew Peterson's album *Love and Thunder* as a worship response to Jesus.

"SERVE HYMN/HOLY IS THE LORD"
BY ANDREW PETERSON

(Song Summary)

My sins, I know, are so obvious and destructive and big that it's overwhelming to think of them.

I've hurt the One who loves me best so deeply—I'm not sure anything can make it right.

But God's love is so powerful, so deep, so all-encompassing that it can overshadow—more like swallow—the destructive consequences of my sin.

His great love for me makes me want to serve him all the days of my life—his fierce rescue of me has given me a treasured hope.

Now I'm learning to appreciate—even treasure—every moment, every breath I take, and every created beauty around me. And that's all because I've tasted his over-shadowing love and grace in my life.

God is so glorious, but in his humility he didn't let his glory be a barrier between us. In his mercy he stooped low to scoop me up.

Jesus…well, I just don't deserve the love of such a glorious King. It makes me want to serve him all the days of my life. It makes me want to gush with praise about him. Only Jesus is good, through and through.

ENDNOTE 1: Mark Galli, *Jesus Mean and Wild: The Unexpected Love of an Untamable God* (Baker Books, 2006), p. 112.
ENDNOTE 2: These questions are taken from *JCQs: 150 Jesus-Centered Questions* by Rick Lawrence (Group Publishing, 2006).
ENDNOTE 3: Annie Dillard, *Teaching a Stone to Talk* (Harper & Row, 1982), p. 52.
ENDNOTE 4: Mark Galli, *Jesus Mean and Wild: The Unexpected Love of an Untamable God* (Baker Books, 2006), p. 112.

IN PURSUIT OF JESUS

WEEK 9: JESUS, THE SLAUGHTERED LAMB

PRIOR TO THIS SESSION

- ▶ Set up a boombox or stereo system to play music.
- ▶ Set up a white board or big pad of paper, along with markers.
- ▶ Set up a VCR or DVD player connected to a TV or a projector to show a film clip.
- ▶ Cue up track 11, "Behold the Lamb of God," on Andrew Peterson's *Behold the Lamb of God* CD for your closing worship.
- ▶ Consider playing John Michael Talbot's album *Empty Canvas* (Sparrow, 1986) in the background while participants look at a print of a painting called *Agnus Dei*. If you can't use this CD, any contemplative instrumental recording will work.
- ▶ Cue up the "death scene" of Obi-Wan Kenobi from the original *Star Wars* film, *Star Wars IV: A New Hope* (from 1:29:53 to 1:32:54 on the DVD).
- ▶ Print a color copy of the painting *Agnus Dei* by Francisco Zurbarán.

  Option 1: Go to www.pursuitofjesus.com, click on the "Agnus Dei" link, and print it on a color printer.

  Option 2: Go to www.art.com and type "Agnus Dei" in the search box. Print the sample image on a color printer.

  Option 3: Use an online search engine for "Agnus Dei by the artist Zurburan," and choose the best image you can find to print.

WELCOME AND INTRODUCTION (10 MINUTES)

After welcoming people to this session, open in prayer. Ask God to allow your eyes and ears to be open to Jesus today.

Then say something like:

> We can describe Jesus in so many ways. It's amazing how many names he's been given in Scripture.

Then ask something like:

▶ **What names of Jesus can you remember?**

Write participants' responses on your white board or pad. Add these names if no one else mentions them:

▶ Lion

▶ Messiah

▶ Master

▶ Teacher

▶ Christ

▶ Son of God

▶ Prophet

▶ Lamb of God

Then say something like:

> Jesus' names symbolize his nature—the essence of who he is. And his names also represent his "work"—his true mission from God. For example, "Rabbi" describes Jesus' nature of truth and his work of teaching.
>
> Today we'll explore what "Lamb of God" says about Jesus' nature and his work. Let's look at a few places in the Bible that describe Jesus as a lamb:
>
> ▶ Isaiah 53:7-8: "He was oppressed and afflicted, yet he did not open his mouth; he was led like a lamb to the slaughter, and as a sheep before her shearers is silent, so he did not open his mouth. By

oppression and judgment he was taken away. And who can speak of his descendants? For he was cut off from the land of the living; for the transgression of my people he was stricken."

▶ John 1:29: "The next day John [the Baptist] saw Jesus coming toward him and said, 'Look, the Lamb of God, who takes away the sin of the world!'"

▶ 1 Peter 1:18-19: "For you know that it was not with perishable things such as silver or gold that you were redeemed from the empty way of life handed down to you from your forefathers, but with the precious blood of Christ, a lamb without blemish or defect."

▶ Revelation 5–7 *(excerpts)*: In the vision John records in the book of Revelation, he hears a mighty angel ask, "Who is worthy to break the seals and open the scroll?" (5:2). He goes on to observe: "Then I saw a Lamb, looking as if it had been slain, standing in the center of the throne, encircled by the four living creatures and the elders" (5:6). And then ends this portion of his vision with: "For the Lamb at the center of the throne will be their shepherd; he will lead them to springs of living water. And God will wipe away every tear from their eyes" (7:17).

THREE VIEWS OF THE SLAUGHTERED LAMB (55 MINUTES)

Tell people that the bulk of this session will be focused on three adventurous experiments in observation. You'll use art, film, and "parable prayers" as jumping-off points to experience Jesus as the "slaughtered Lamb" (by the way, it's important not to back away from the word "slaughtered," even though it's a strong word).

Say something like:

Now let's jump into three different explorations of Jesus. First we'll study the painting *Agnus Dei* by the artist Francisco Zurbarán. (Hold up a print of the painting for people to see.) Zurbarán painted this in the early 1600s, and the original now hangs in the Museo Del Prado in Madrid.

After you give each person a print of *Agnus Dei, say something like*:

I'd like you to simply stare at the print for the next five minutes or so. That's right—five straight minutes of staring at the painting. I realize this will be an uncomfortably long time, but just play with this experience by following my directions. Resist the urge to look away or to look at others during this five-minute time. Simply ask God to give you insight into Jesus as you look at the painting.

As you study the painting, think about three questions, listed in your booklet on page 69:

▶ **What do you notice?**

▶ **What do you see that supports your perceptions, knowledge, and experience of Jesus?**

▶ **What do you see that does not support your perceptions, knowledge, and experience of Jesus?**

After five minutes, *say something like:*

Name at least one thing you learned from your insights into the painting.

"Agnus Dei"

, Resignation

• Cords cutting into skin

• Horns — male + fierce

• Not fighting

• Eyes averted

• He's clean at this point

I don't experience Jesus as "soft + resigned."

THE RULES OF ENGAGEMENT

Whenever you gather input from the whole group—either from a question you ask or as they report back on discussions they have—use these tips to remember how to prime the discussion, ask follow-up questions, and engage the responses you get back:

1. Embrace every answer. Write a condensed version of each one on your white board or pad.
2. If an answer seems vague, confusing, wrong, or sounds like the Sunday school "right" answer, follow up with one of these go-deeper comments or questions:
   - ▶ "Please say more about what you mean."
   - ▶ "I've never thought of that before—could you explain more?"
   - ▶ "That seems to contradict what we commonly believe—could you be more specific?"
   - ▶ "That's the answer we expect. How would you explain that to someone who doesn't know the 'expected' answer?"
3. If an answer is surprising or insightful, ask the person to say a little more (unless the answer was detailed in the first place). You can ask others in the group to expand on that answer, too.
4. When someone specifically connects with where the study is headed, highlight that answer as important to pay attention to.
5. Aim for developing an atmosphere that resembles a good conversation, where you and other group members interact all the time with what someone says.

After you gather at least one response from each person, move into the second exploration.

SHOW FILM CLIP

You'll show the "death scene" of Obi-Wan Kenobi from the original *Star Wars* film. *Say something like:*

For the few who've never seen this movie, or in case you've forgotten the story, this scene shows the old master "Jedi Knight" Obi-Wan Kenobi battling with Darth Vader, the personification of evil. Obi-Wan is the spiritual leader of the rebel movement fighting against the evil empire.

In this scene, Obi-Wan looks for Darth Vader to fight him while his young friends in the rebellion try to rescue princess Leia from imprisonment and torture.

Play the "death scene" of Obi-Wan Kenobi—1:29:53 to 1:32:54 on the DVD.

After the clip, instruct people to get into trios. Then take seven minutes to answer these questions:

▶ What did you notice in this scene that sheds light on Jesus as the "Lamb of God"?

▶ What in this scene supports your perceptions, knowledge, and experience of Jesus?

▶ What in this scene does not support your perceptions, knowledge, and experience of Jesus?

When time is up, ask a spokesperson from each trio to report on their discussions. Remember to use The Rules of Engagement. After each trio responds, move into the third exploration.

In this segment, people will wander close to your meeting place and ask God to show them a parable of the slaughtered Lamb—Jesus.

Say something like:

You can go anywhere you want for the next seven minutes, as long as it's not too far from our meeting area. Wander until something captures your eye or ear. This might be as simple as noticing what captures your attention as you walk—a sound, a sight, or anything. As soon as you notice something, stop and simply ask God to show you if he's providing a parable that offers insight into Jesus as the slaughtered Lamb.

You might find something or not—don't worry about it. This isn't a test. We're just playing. Yet don't rush the process. If you notice something, wait in silence long enough to give yourself and God a chance to see a parable of Jesus as the slaughtered Lamb. Just wait on God.

Make sure people know exactly what time to return. When they gather in your meeting area again, *ask something like:*

> ▶ **What did you notice, and how might it be a parable for the slaughtered Lamb?**

Remember to use The Rules of Engagement. It's likely that at least one person in your group will come back with a parable. But if no one does, or if many people didn't sense anything on their walk, back up your emphasis about "playing" with this. This isn't some kind of a test of faith—it's adventuring with God. Affirm participants' willingness to open themselves, and mention that it sometimes takes time to get used to interacting with God this way.

It would be a good idea to try this experience yourself—either during the study or prior to it. That way, you can offer your own experience, and your own parable, as an example here. For those who don't come back with a parable, you can still explore what the experience was like for them. Sometimes people actually find a parable but don't recognize it at the time.

CLOSING WORSHIP RESPONSE (10 MINUTES)

Jesus gave up his life of his own will. No one took it from him. Give a brief overview of Jesus' path to the cross by drawing a line on your white board or pad that angles up toward an apex or point, then angles down again.

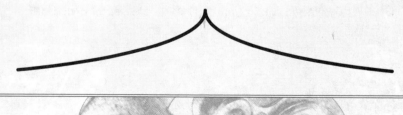

Say something like:

The beginning point on this line is Jesus' birth in Bethlehem. Let's follow Jesus up the line toward his decision to give himself over to the cross. In this part of Jesus' journey, he reveals who he is, but consciously does things to delay his arrest and execution *(mark an X at the beginning of the line).*

In John 8:20-21, Jesus reveals his true identity. But the authorities don't seize him. This happens many times on his upward journey to a turning point in his public ministry. Here, in the middle of the upward line, he tells his followers that he's going where "you cannot come." Where is Jesus going that we can't come? To the altar to be slaughtered. He's the Lamb—alone in this mission. This explains his many betrayals, his loneliness in Gethsemane, and his aloneness on the cross. We aren't asked to go where Jesus goes because we can't— *only* the Lamb can go where Jesus is going.

At the top of this upward journey, Jesus reaches a major turning point *(mark an X at the top of the line).* Here, Jesus determines when the time is right to move toward death.

In Matthew 12:8-16, Jesus heals a man with a withered hand on the Sabbath. He appears to do this to purposely antagonize the powerful Jewish leaders of Jerusalem. Only when Jesus enters Jerusalem—the seat of political power—does he become a real threat. This is the start of his downward journey to the cross.

(Now point to the downward sloping line, and draw another X at the end of the line.) Now Jesus intentionally does things to get himself killed. In John 11, the high priest Caiaphas hatches the death plot against Jesus. Caiaphas says: "It is expedient for you that one man die for the people" (NAS). And later, in John 18:19-24, Jesus seals his own death

by purposely provoking the high priest. Finally, in Matthew 27:11-26, Pilate tries hard to release Jesus, but Jesus outsmarts him and makes sure he will be executed.

Jesus didn't come to abolish the law, but to fulfill it. He didn't come to abolish the brutal system of animal sacrifice; he came to place the once-and-final sacrifice on the altar. To close, let's listen to a song by Andrew Peterson.

Play the song "Behold the Lamb of God" from Andrew Peterson's album of the same name. Then close in prayer. Remember that prayer is conversation, so simply talk to Jesus about the experience you just walked through. This is a great place to thank him for

- willingly and shrewdly choosing his own death as a once-and-for-all blood sacrifice for our sins.
- trusting his Father through the agony of the cross, when everyone (including his Father) had left him alone.

"BEHOLD THE LAMB OF GOD" BY ANDREW PETERSON

(Song Summary)

Stare long and hard at Jesus, who gave himself up to be slaughtered on the cross—of his own free will.

His sacrifice gives us hope and life and lights our darkness. His sacrifice has taken away the penalty of death for our sins.

In our wayward acts of betrayal, we've strayed so far and damaged our own hearts so deeply. We so desperately need a rescuer.

And Jesus is that rescuer! He's our only hope. We're entirely dependent on his goodness toward us. We could never ask him to do what he did willingly—to give up all he had and endure the torture of the cross on our behalf.

There is no one like Jesus!

IN PURSUIT OF JESUS

WEEK 10: JESUS, POST-RESURRECTION

PRIOR TO THIS SESSION

- Set up a boombox or stereo system to play music.
- Set up a white board or big pad of paper, along with markers.
- Set up a VCR or DVD player connected to a TV or a projector to show a film clip.
- Cue up track 5, "God's Own Fool," on Disc 2 of Michael Card's *The Life* CD for your opening worship song.
- You'll also play track 15, "Joy in the Journey," on Disc 2 of Michael Card's *The Life* CD for your closing worship song.
- Cue up the scene from *A Christmas Carol* (the 1984 version starring George C. Scott) to the scene early in the film where the ghost of Jacob Marley confronts Scrooge (from 19:45 to 23:37 on the DVD).

WELCOME AND INTRODUCTION (10 MINUTES)

After you welcome everyone, *say something like:*

Remember our overarching pursuit? We're trying to answer Jesus when he asks us, "Who do you say I am?" To begin our time together today, let's listen to singer Michael Card take a shot at answering that question in the song titled "God's Own Fool."

Play Michael Card's song "God's Own Fool." Direct participants to the song summary printed on page 76, or you can go to www.pursuitofjesus.com for a link to the actual lyrics online.

After the song is over, *ask something like:*

▶ **We almost always think of foolishness as a bad thing. How and why did Michael Card use it as a positive description of Jesus in this song?**

THE RULES OF ENGAGEMENT

Whenever you gather input from the whole group—either from a question you ask or as they report back on discussions they have—use these tips to remember how to prime the discussion, ask follow-up questions, and engage the responses you get back:

1. Embrace every answer. Write a condensed version of each one on your white board or pad.
2. If an answer seems vague, confusing, wrong, or sounds like the Sunday school "right" answer, follow up with one of these go-deeper comments or questions:
   ▶ "Please say more about what you mean."
   ▶ "I've never thought of that before—could you explain more?"
   ▶ "That seems to contradict what we commonly believe—could you be more specific?"
   ▶ "That's the answer we expect. How would you explain that to someone who doesn't know the 'expected' answer?"
3. If an answer is surprising or insightful, ask the person to say a little more (unless the answer was detailed in the first place). You can ask others in the group to expand on that answer, too.
4. When someone specifically connects with where the study is headed, highlight that answer as important to pay attention to.
5. Aim for developing an atmosphere that resembles a good conversation, where you and other group members interact all the time with what someone says.

After you gather several responses, draw a line down the middle of your white board or pad. On the left side of the line, list all of the session titles the class has completed (see below).

▶ Who Do You Say I Am?
▶ Jesus Defines "Good"
▶ Jesus and His Parables
▶ Jesus and the Desperate People
▶ Jesus and His Family
▶ Jesus and Satan's Family
▶ Jesus and His True Mission
▶ Jesus Acting Supernaturally
▶ Jesus, the Slaughtered Lamb

Then, on the other side of the line, write the heading "Jesus, Post-Resurrection."

Now say something like:

So far in this pursuit we've focused on what Jesus said and did on his way to the cross—during his earthly ministry. In this last session, we'll look at Jesus' strange and mysterious behavior after his resurrection. Really, this is a kind of "afterlife" for Jesus, and we should be particularly interested because we know next to nothing about life on the other side of death. Mostly, we're scared by it. We're always frightened by the unknown.

SHOW FILM CLIP

Say something like:

What's on the other side of death? A famous writer wrote a famous story that, in part, tried to answer that question. Most of us have seen some rendition of *A Christmas Carol* by Charles Dickens. In the scene we're about to watch, the ghost of Ebenezer Scrooge's old partner, Jacob Marley, comes back to haunt Scrooge—to scare him into changing his ways and to warn him that he'll be visited by three spirits during the night.

Show the scene of the ghost of Marley confronting Scrooge. Play 19:45–23:37 on the DVD.

After the clip, *ask something like:*

▶ **How plausible, or not, is Dickens' picture of the afterlife?**

No need to drill deep into this question—just gather a few quick responses.

THE THREE QUESTIONS (15 MINUTES)
Say something like:

In this last session, we'll pursue Jesus' post-resurrection behavior individually, in groups, and all together. First, an individual adventure.

We'll all be focusing on three chapters in the Bible: one from Luke and two from John. The passages are Luke 24 and John 20–21. Please mark these somehow in your Bibles right now. I want you to read quickly through these chapters, looking for answers to your assigned question. You'll each have one of three questions to answer as you read.

Number off the participants from one to three.

The Ones will answer the question "What did Jesus *really* say?" They should filter their study of the assigned passages through the lens of this question. Ask them to imagine that Jesus said these things with a totally different inflection or tone than they've always assumed. For example, if they've always assumed Jesus said something in a serious tone, how would it change the meaning if they assumed he said it smiling or with laughter in his voice?

The Twos will answer the question "What did Jesus *really* do?" They should filter their study of the assigned passages through the lens of this question. Ask them to imagine that Jesus did these things for totally different reasons than they've always assumed. So if they've always imagined that Jesus was mad at Thomas for doubting him, how would it change the meaning of his response to Thomas if they imagined Jesus was amused at his doubts instead?

The Threes will answer the question "How did others *really* react to Jesus?" They should filter their study of the assigned passages through the lens of this question. Ask them to imagine that they themselves were among the people experiencing Jesus in these passages.

After 10 minutes or so, gather all the Ones at one table or in a circle together. Do the same for the Twos and Threes. Tell them now to talk about their insights, truths, common threads, surprises, and profound ah-ha moments from their personal study. Then they should come up with a list or a sentence that they all agree answers their assigned question:

• (Group 1) Why did Jesus say these things? (Possible sentence: "Jesus said these things because, in part, he wanted to assure his followers that his absence on the earth was leading to something really good.")

• (Group 2) Why did Jesus do these things? (Possible sentence: "Jesus wanted to show his followers that he had entered a new and richer kind of life, the same life he intends us to share with him.")

• (Group 3) Why did others react to Jesus the ways they did? (Possible sentence: "Others reacted to Jesus the way they did because what was happening was so outside their expectations and life experience that it was hard to get their minds around it.")

After 10 minutes or so, ask a spokesperson from each table or group to report on the group's answer to the assigned question. Remember to use The Rules of Engagement. In addition, after each group shares, ask the rest of the group to react and interact with what's been said. Prompt them by asking these questions (*you don't have to ask all of them every time*):

▶ **What's something you like about this group's answer?**
▶ **What's something you don't like, or disagree with?**

- ▶ What's missing from their answer?
- ▶ From what the group shared, what really sticks out to you about Jesus?

Be sure to ask the following question after every group shares:

- ▶ If we only had this information about Jesus, how would we answer his question "Who do you say I am?"

As you lead this discussion for each assigned question, make sure to add your own perspectives and insights along the way. Remember the goal: to answer Jesus' question "Who do you say I am?"

ANSWERING THE BIG QUESTION (15 MINUTES)

Collect all of the answers into one answer to Jesus' question: Who do you say I am? Ask participants to suggest the answer, and work with it until you all agree on it. Write it on your white board or pad.

Then stand in a circle and hold hands. Invite anyone who wants to thank Jesus for who he is and how he revealed himself during this pursuit to pray. Then close this time by praying yourself.

Have people continue to hold hands as you play the closing song for this 10-week pursuit, Michael Card's song "Joy in the Journey."

"GOD'S OWN FOOL" BY MICHAEL CARD

(Song Summary)

I've always thought of Jesus as the wisest man who ever lived, but God himself has described wisdom as seeming "foolish" to most people—that means Jesus was the biggest fool of all!

Pretty much everyone in Jesus' life thought, at one time or another, he was crazy. He said and did things that made absolutely no sense to people.

We're all like little children who think we know it all already—but Jesus cured our blindness by "playing the fool." For example, he showed his strength by choosing weakness. His example draws us to him—makes us want to follow him. Something in us is "foolish" as well—we recognize God's foolishness is really the deepest wisdom, and we want to live as he lives.

To gain everything—to live as a fool for God—we must die to our own wisdom, our own self-sufficiency, and give everything over to Jesus. When we do, we'll find ourselves living in a faith adventure, and we'll know what it is to suffer on his behalf.

If we give up our "right" to understand everything—if, instead, we act on our passionate attraction to Jesus and commit ourselves to believing in his "foolish wisdom," our eyes will be opened to his truth.

We can't help but follow Jesus, because he's planted in our hearts a love for his truth, his goodness, his wisdom.

"JOY IN THE JOURNEY" BY MICHAEL CARD

(Song Summary)

Life isn't just about the "end"—there's so much joy locked up in our along-the-way experiences. For example, God's truths are like a light in the darkness. And our lives are full of mystery and adventure. And when we do what God asks us to do, we experience a deep sense of freedom.

If you're looking for forgiveness, you'll find it when you believe in the Forgiver. And if you're looking for a light at the end of your personal tunnel, you'll find it in the Father of Lights.

So for everyone who's committed him- or herself to God—who now shares his eternal life even while you're stuck dealing with the impact of sin in your life—don't forget God's promise to you, that you'll live with him as his own son or daughter forevermore. Of course, a life committed to following Jesus won't be easy, but don't forget how far you had wandered from his love.

It's worth repeating…Life isn't just about the "end"—there's so much joy locked up in our along-the-way experiences. For example, God's truths are like a light in the darkness. And our lives are full of mystery and adventure. And when we do what God asks us to do, we experience a deep sense of freedom.

NOTES:

NOTES:

NOTES:

NOTES:

NOTES:

NOTES:

NOTES:

NOTES: